Growing Up Writing

MINI-LESSONS FOR EMERGENT AND BEGINNING WRITERS

Connie Campbell Dierking

Sherra Ann Jones

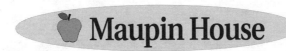

Growing Up Writing:
Mini-Lessons for Emergent and Beginning Writers

Cover Art: Gaye Dell
Layout Design: Maria Messenger
Editor: Mark Devish

Library of Congress Cataloging-in-Publication Data

Dierking, Connie Campbell, 1956-
  Growing up writing : mini-lessons for emergent and beginning writers /
Connie Campbell Dierking, Sherra Ann Jones.
    p. cm.
  ISBN 0-929895-71-1
  1. English language--Composition and exercises--Study and teaching
(Preschool) 2. Language arts (Kindergarten) I. Jones, Sherra Ann,
1961- II. Title.
  LB1140.5.L3D54 2003
  372.62'3--dc21

                                                    2003011660

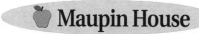 Maupin House

Maupin House Publishing, Inc.
PO Box 90148
Gainesville, FL 32607
1-800-524-0634 / 352-373-5588
352-373-5546 (fax)
www.maupinhouse.com
info@maupinhouse.com

Publishing Professional Resources that Improve Classroom Performance

The images used in Print Awareness Mini-Lesson 13 were obtained from IMSI's MasterClips Collection, 1895 Francisco Blvd. East, San Rafael, CA 94901-5506, USA.

Dedication

To Jessica Noelle, Rachael Marie,
Madeline June, and Andrea JoAnn:
Where inspiration begins

S.A.J.
C.C.D.

Table of Contents

Section Two: Operational Mini-Lessons (continued)

Section Three: Print Awareness Mini-Lessons

Section Four: Foundational Mini-Lessons

Section Five: Craft Mini-Lessons

Acknowledgments

Writing a book required the assistance and support of many people. The completion of this book required a debt of gratitude to the educators that surround us in our work. The contributions of these role models continue to be reflected in our daily practice.

A special thanks goes to the folks in the Reading and Language Arts Department of the Pinellas County School System. Your visionary approach to the teaching of early writers gave us a foundation from which to grow. The training opportunities you provided promoted our growth as life-long learners. For this we will be eternally grateful.

Thank you to Marianne Easton, Early Childhood Supervisor for Pinellas County Schools. Your support of kindergarten teachers through materials and training is exemplary.

The teachers and staff of Curtis Fundamental Elementary continue to support the teaching of writing at all levels. Thank you for allowing us to be a part of your community of learners. A special, heartfelt thank you goes to our principal, Kathy Duncan, whose positive reinforcement and belief in us continues to inspire us to move forward as educators.

To Kirk Reinking: we owe you tremendously for your technological expertise, especially since we have none!

To the parents of our students: your involvement does make a difference. Thank you for going the extra mile!

To our students: you are a constant inspiration. The gift of your words brings us energy and enlightens our world. Thank you for letting us use your ideas and for always showing us how you learn best.

Thanks to Kim and Peggy Warmoltz, Lasting Impressions Photography, Tarpon Springs, FL, for our author photo.

Finally, to our immediate families: thank you for your patience. Your recognition of the importance of this project helped lessen the guilt of the time spent away from you!

Writing in the Kindergarten Classroom

CHAPTER ONE

The Importance of Writing Instruction in Emergent Literacy

"Writing is the foundation of reading; it may be the most basic way to learn about reading...when writers read, they use insights they have acquired when they compose...when our students write, they learn how reading is put together because they can do it. They learn the essence of print."

When Writers Read, Jane Hansen, 1987

Introduction

We believe that kindergartners—and emergent writers of any age—should be treated like genuine authors and taught in a manner that respects their abilities while empowering their advancements.

It's a simple idea that might sound impossible to some and frighteningly difficult to others, but really, it is a simple idea. Implementing it is surprisingly easy, and the results of doing so are compelling and diverse. It boils down to this: we ground our kindergartners in the same writing craft and process workshops that are prevalent in the classrooms of upper-grade students. We know that writer's workshop—often reserved for more advanced grades—offers the most effective environment for the teaching of writing. There is no reason to withhold it from young students.

Workshops at this level need to be tailored to your students' abilities. Skills that are taken for granted in higher grades (how to move between the different stages of writer's workshop, what to do if your pencil breaks during independent practice, where you begin writing on the page) need to be explicitly taught to emergent writers. The connection between reading and writing needs to be emphasized. The workshop model—combined with our system of categorizing mini-lessons—offers the flexibility that teachers of young writers need to focus their lessons.

The purpose of this book is to share some of the more useful fruits that we've gathered during our teaching journeys. We have addressed it to kindergarten teachers, but the lessons we've included can be easily adapted to any classroom with students that are just beginning to understand literacy. It is our hope that it will help all teachers of emergent and beginning writers.

When working under the structure of a daily writer's workshop, emergent and beginning writers will astound their audiences. Their accomplishments have no limits: enjoy their stories, applaud their efforts. Let them write, every day. The pay off is priceless.

Writing in the Kindergarten Classroom

It's hard to remember a time when we didn't teach writing to our kindergartners. Our memories of the last fifteen years are filled with students hovering over journals, their pencils scratching their thoughts onto paper. We remember scores of proud authors reading what they had written, and writer-ly conversations blossoming as their peers discussed their pieces. Our memories include a blur of young faces as they left us armed for the challenges of the upper-elementary grades with well developed literacy skills.

However, the truth is there were times, especially early on, when the atmosphere was filled with frustration and confusion instead of the stuff that happy memories are made of. In the beginning, we dove in without considering the purpose of a framework. We were trying to build a writing community and put processes in place outside of a structure that could offer the stability of a scaffold. Mini-lessons on labeling pictures would get lost in discussions on managing materials. Meaningful peer feedback was scarce and often misdirected. Our well intended discussions often seemed to spin out of control. A writer's workshop that exploded into ninety minutes frustrated everyone.

Still, we remained excited about the progress our students made. Children who started the year scribbling were soon using mock or random letters. Artists were labeling their pictures, lists were being made, letters were put together to form words, and words strung together to construct sentences. Our students were understanding the purpose of writing as communication.

We made note of the simplest things. Praise for our students' temporary spellings was rewarded with confident attempts at description and elaboration. As the year progressed, so did their skills. Many were able to write a simple story with a beginning, middle, and end, as well as use some specific details with good word choice, elaboration, and focus.

We were convinced: kindergartners rapidly benefit from exposure to the fundamentals of writing craft and process. Every writer, no matter how young, benefits from knowing that *all* writers go through a multi-step process when creating a given piece. Every writer gains confidence and flexibility by learning specific targeted skills that help them handle specific writing situations.

In our kindergarten workshops, we spend most of our time showing students how to identify ideas to write about, and how to move those ideas into print. Almost all of what we do in kindergarten is a first write. Emergent writers *can* revise and make their pieces better, as well as edit for simple rules such as capital letters and periods: we practice these stages of the writing process, but they are not the main focus of our writing program.

We want our students to learn that two words on a sheet of paper do not constitute a finished piece of writing. Good writing takes time. Emergent writers need to know that up front.

Our intent is not to spend the majority of our writing time moving a piece towards publishing. Our intent is to practice the use of specific targeted skills in authentic pieces generated from topics of student choice. Writer's workshop is the ideal vehicle for practicing any skill related to writing craft or process. Kindergarten is the ideal time to introduce it.

No matter what stage of literacy you are addressing, you should be using the structure of a daily writer's workshop to support your students in their development. If you are not, may we recommend the bibliography found on page 129? From Brian Camborne's conditions of learning through the work of Donald Graves, there is plenty of compelling research to support using a daily writer's workshop to immerse your students into the writing process and the fundamentals of writing craft.

The Reading-Writing Connection

We expected positive results. After implementing writer's workshop in our kindergarten classrooms, we knew we would see a marked improvement in our students' writing performance. And we saw it. Before moving to first grade, nearly every student had met or exceeded the writing expectations for our county.

What we weren't expecting—what really blew us away—was the almost magical progress these same students made in reading.

Nothing about our instructional strategies for reading had changed from the previous year. We continued to use Best Practices, including shared and guided reading, word work, and read-alouds. We had incorporated a balanced literacy approach in our daily reading instruction. Our students were spending the same amount of time reading independently and in partnerships just as the students before them had.

However, our assessments indicated that our students were making huge leaps in reading. Children were rapidly becoming efficient word decoders. Reading levels were escalating. Students were engaging in authentic conversations about read-alouds. They were noticing author styles and offering specific feedback regarding word choice, illustration techniques, and author craft.

We were stumped. In meetings, we sheepishly accepted congratulations for our students' accelerated performance. But we were unsure exactly what we had done. Why *were* our students performing so well in reading? No strategic changes had been made, no additional time had been given to reading instruction. Class size was the same, student demographics were similar, and their ability levels were comparable to previous years.

Finally, it started to come together. The variable that had changed was the inclusion of direct writing instruction.

An Integrated Approach

We examined our district expectations, which outline specific goals that must be mastered by the end of kindergarten. As with most kindergarten programs, they included the following: awareness of print, phonemic awareness, letter/sound correspondence, concept of letter/word, vocabulary, sequence of events, sight words, story elements, voice/print match, and concept development. These are all necessary skills for becoming a proficient reader. They are also necessary skills for becoming a proficient writer. Teaching children to become word solvers in writing supports their development as word solvers in reading.

We began to think of it as pouring information from a pitcher of knowledge. From the same container you can fill two cups. We were convinced that students exposed to a writing routine in kindergarten would experience less reluctance and fear as they honed their reading and writing skills.

We realized that reading and writing are so connected, especially for the very young student, that it only made sense to use a teaching model that provided for simultaneous instruction. Once again, writer's workshop is that model.

CHAPTER TWO

Writer's Workshop—
The Framework for Teaching Writing

Writer's Workshop: Predictably Effective

A workshop is, by definition, a place where raw materials are used to build something. Writer's workshop provides the materials, instruction, and support your students need to build a piece of writing.

This chapter is intended to give you an overview of the workshop process. Again, please refer to the bibliography (page 129) for suggested reading on the effectiveness of this teaching method.

A successful writer's workshop should include three parts: **the mini-lesson**, **independent practice with conferencing**, and **sharing**. Include all three in your classroom. Children learn best when information is presented in a predictable structure. Consistently including all three steps provides the predictability young children need to hone their writing skills.

Writer's Workshop
45 minutes

5 to 10 minutes   5 to 10 minutes

Sharing
- notice
- question
- personal connect

Mini-Lesson
- connection
- teach
- engage
- link

**Independent Practice
with Conferencing**
- research
- decide
- teach

20 to 30 minutes

Part One: The Mini-Lesson

Direct instruction—in the form of a mini-lesson—is the first part of each writer's workshop. A mini-lesson is the modeling and demonstration of a target skill: it is your lesson plan for teaching writing.

The mini-lesson is especially important in the kindergarten classroom. *Any* skill that needs to be taught to your students can be taught under the structure of a mini-lesson. Don't be afraid to use the mini-lesson to teach even the simplest skills. Young students need direct instruction in the things that are not familiar to them. If they are having trouble returning their journals to the proper places, design a mini-lesson to reinforce the skill.

A mini-lesson does not have to be on a grand academic topic. It is simply a teaching structure that allows you to keep your students engaged and focused on what you need them to understand.

Chapter 3 covers the mini-lesson in detail. Included is our classification of mini-lessons by the function they serve in the kindergarten classroom. **Operational Mini-Lessons** cover skills related to the management of classroom processes, materials, and spaces. **Print Awareness Mini-Lessons** cover the mechanics of writing (letter/sound correspondence, orientation of writing on the page, punctuation rules, the use of temporary spelling, etc). These lessons directly address the reading-writing connection. **Foundational Mini-Lessons** encourage the content of your students' writing. Finally, our **Craft Mini-Lessons** address the skills students need to craft their writing so it rises above the level of mere acceptability. These lessons focus on details, the use of active verbs, elaboration, etc.

Also in chapter 3, we answer some of the most common questions teachers have about the mini-lesson.

Part Two: Independent Practice with Conferencing

Independent Practice

Practice makes perfect! Children relate to that phrase quite easily when you remind them of how often they had to practice riding a two-wheeler or tying a shoe before they became proficient. We often ask if they think Shaquille O'Neil is a great basketball player because he only watched other boys play basketball or if Michelle Kwan is an accomplished ice skater because she watched ice skating on television. Their answer is an emphatic "NO!"

The same thing is true of writing. To become a proficient writer you have to practice writing. Part 2 of writer's workshop provides that essential practice time.

The largest portion of your workshop time should be spent in independent practice. Children must be given a large amount of uninterrupted time to practice their writing if you except them to improve. At the beginning of the school year, this time will only be about ten minutes. As they build stamina and fluency, increase the amount of practice time. By mid-year, your students should be writing for a period of twenty to thirty minutes.

Independent practice is not the time to prescribe writing topics. Your students should be allowed to freely write about any topic they choose. Likewise, students should not be required to attempt to use the skill that you taught during that day's particular mini-lesson. This time should be reserved for your students to flex their writing muscles in any way they choose.

What Does Independent Practice Look Like?

Independent practice looks like an entire class actively engaged in writing. It is up to you to make the decisions that will support your students in this goal. At the beginning of the year you'll need to decide where you want your students to practice. Will they practice writing at their tables or desks? Maybe it works better if they write on the floor or in specified writing dens. Will students be allowed to use resources such as alphabet strips or literature books? Where will they find these so they don't disturb others? These are all important decisions that will need to be made in order for your workshop to function effectively.

In Connie's classroom, the children are dismissed from the floor after the mini-lesson to a writing space of their choosing. They are allowed to write at a desk, at a table, in a chair, or on the floor. The spot doesn't matter as long as each student takes responsibility for his behavior and spends this time writing. If a student chooses to write on the floor, she grabs a clipboard from the bin and uses it for a writing surface. Students are allowed to sit in someone else's desk during this time if they choose. Again, wherever they feel comfortable enough to think and put thoughts to paper is an acceptable writing den. These dens change from day to day, but permanent dens can be assigned.

At the beginning of the year, Sherra dismisses her children to their desks to write. As the year progresses, writing on the floor or in specified writing dens usually becomes an option.

See Operational Mini-Lesson 7 for a lesson in managing the transition into independent practice time.

Silent vs. Quiet Writing

We divide independent practice into two categories: silent writing and quiet writing. We give our students equal time for each type. **Silent writing** begins the practice. Children are not permitted to move around the room or converse with each other during silent writing. We use timers to measure the period during which students write silently. At the beginning of the year you will have to be very stringent about enforcing proper behavior during silent writing. Your students will learn that silent writing is a sacred time for writers, and that interruption is not acceptable.

We play soft music during silent writing, usually classical or instrumental. Research supports the notion of music stimulating both sides of the brain to make it work more effectively. Anything soothing and calm will help the thoughts flow. Music is also an auditory reminder that only writing should be taking place.

When the timer goes off, the children are free to move around the classroom. It has now become **quiet writing** time. During quiet writing, your students are allowed to work with other students. Sharing a piece with a friend for feedback, looking up a word in a class dictionary, or moving closer to the word wall are all acceptable during quiet writing. The hum of voices will let an outsider know that a shift was made in the workshop that was not present before the timer bell.

Operational Mini-Lesson 6 provides a lesson on how your students can learn the behaviors acceptable during silent writing and quiet writing.

Conferencing

What is the teacher doing while the class is engaged in independent practice? You are conferencing with students individually or in small groups.

We begin the student scaffold for understanding the concept of conferencing with a story about a parent/teacher conference. Even the youngest students easily understand that a grown-up who lives with them usually comes to school at least once a year to talk with their teacher. "This meeting time is called 'a conference.' When Jessica's mommy comes to school to meet with Mrs. Jones she wants to hear about Jessica and all her strengths. And Jessica's mommy also wants to hear some feedback about what Jessica could do to move herself forward as a learner and how she can help Jessica do that."

Explain to your students that writing conferences are like parent/teacher conferences: they are little conversations between the teacher and her students that are focused on their writing.

There are three different types of conferences. Try to include each in your teaching strategies throughout the year. The first type focuses on the content of a student's writing. During a **content conference**, encourage your students to elaborate and to get their thoughts down on paper. The second type of conference actually teaches students a new strategy they can use to further develop their writing. You might notice that a child is using several descriptive words in a series. During a **strategy conference**, you could teach him how to use commas to separate his words. Finally, helping students do something that they are already doing, but better, is the foundation for an effective **coaching conference**. Moving information around for improved focus or suggestions for inserting a simile or metaphor would be example topics in a coaching conference.

Conference Basics

Students need to know that they have an audience who will be reading what they write. They need to be assured that you will be paying attention to their writing and giving them feedback.

Preparation for a conference—including deciding on which type of conference to use—should begin with research on the writer. Look at what they are doing during independent practice. Are they staring into space, scribbling, labeling pictures, or writing a sentence but leaving no spaces?

Remember you can't teach everything at once. In a single piece of writing, you may notice problems with spacing, ending sounds, conventions, and focus. Pick one teaching point and be explicit!

After you have decided which problem to address, teach the writer. Try to teach a process or strategy that will last well beyond the piece of writing. If you continually teach to each specific piece of writing, your students will not become independent writers. They will not have the strategies to solve writing problems on their own and will look to you to "fix" their piece. Remember you are teaching the writer not the writing. Whatever skill you teach in a conference, the student must try it. It is not an option!

Conferencing gives you, the teacher, evidence of whether or not your students are applying the skills you have been teaching in your mini-lessons. If you have taught several lessons on leaving spaces between words, but during conferencing notice that you need to keep re-teaching this concept to your class, it's time to admit that the skill is still not sticking. You need to address spaces again.

What Does Conferencing Sound Like?

Teachers often wonder what to say during conference time. Before you begin, compare your expectations to what you see on your emergent writer's page. How can you help move their writing forward? A great opening line for a conference is simple: "Tell me about the writing work you are doing today." It will provide more information than "Can you read your story to me?"

A strategy conference might sound like this:

Teacher: Emily, tell me what writing work you are doing today.

Emily: I am drawing a rainbow and this is the sun and this is me.

Teacher: I see the rainbow takes up most of the picture. That must have been really special when you saw that rainbow.

Emily: It was.

Teacher: What were you thinking when you saw it?

Emily: I was thinking it was really big and I wondered if there was really gold at the end like my dad said.

Teacher: I only see the rainbow, I don't see the gold. Does that mean you decided there was no gold at the rainbow?

Emily: Oh, I think there is gold!

Teacher: Where on your rainbow would you find the gold?

Emily: Right here. (She points to the end of the rainbow.)

Teacher: So do you think your reader will want to see that gold too?

(Emily nods her head.)

Teacher: I'm hearing you say the gold at the end of the rainbow is important to your story. Add the gold and any other details you remember.

The teacher in this scenario determined the writing work that Emily was doing involved telling a story through pictures. She then gave Emily positive feedback on her pictures. By encouraging Emily to share her story verbally, and then to add details to her picture, the teacher has given Emily a strategy for elaborating her next piece of writing. The teacher could have given instruction on letter/sound correspondence or labeling but chose today to stick only to thinking about details in her writing.

What follows is an example of a content conference. Included is the actual piece the student was working on. His revision follows on page 13.

Teacher: Tell me what you're working on.

Kalvin: I'm writing about going to the beach.

Teacher: Wow! It looks like you did quite a few different things that day. Let's count the things you did 1) built a sandcastle 2) went to McDonald's 3) ate lunch on the beach 4) ate dinner at home 5) took a shower and 6) put on your pajamas.

That's a lot of things to write about in one piece. Let's get focused by zooming in on the one activity that was the most interesting for you that day. Tell me which activity was the most fun?

Kalvin: Building the sandcastle was the most fun.

Teacher: Great! Circle the word 'sandcastle' in your piece. That will help you stay focused. Tell me more about building the sandcastle. What did it look like? How did you build it?

Kalvin: I pushed the sand up to make a mountain, and then I put a flag on top.

Teacher: Tell me more.

Kalvin: I made a moat around it and I put a piece of wood for a bridge. I put water in the moat.

Teacher: How long do you think the sandcastle lasted?

Kalvin: I don't know.

Teacher: When you rewrite this piece, do you think you should keep the title "The Beach Party"? Could you call it something else?

Kalvin: Maybe I could call it "The Sandcastle" since it'll just be about my sandcastle?

Teacher: I think that's a great idea. Remember, when you rewrite this piece, stay focused. Write only about the sandcastle. Keep up the good work. I can't wait to read it again!

Small Group Conferences

There will be times when you notice that a group of three or four students is experiencing a common problem in their writing. It is quite effective to call that group to a central area and conference with them all together. They will benefit from seeing each other's writing and hearing the feedback presented to the group. For example, if you notice a small group of students leaving off ending sounds, you could include them in a small-group conference. Rewrite some words on chart paper and have the group help each other complete the ending sounds. Small-group conferences are great for time management, and for reinforcing student skills.

The sandcastle

I Made a sorndCastle

at the bech. I posht

Sard up to Make a

Moutan. I fownd

Flag And star it

on top of the

Castle. I dug

a Mote around

the Castle. thin I

Fild it with Watr.

the Laske thething I

did was lay a Pes of wood

acros the Mote. it looked

Like a briige. I wann

have Log it stod

Keeping a Record of Conferences

How to record your conferences with students is a personal decision. But you need to devise a method that is easy to implement and doesn't interfere with your teaching style. Some teachers use simple boxes with a plus on one side of the child's name and a delta on the other side. They quickly jot notes on the appropriate side as needed. Some teachers use sticky notes to record writing behaviors. Later, they move the stickies to a master sheet to be kept in the child's cumulative record.

A written record allows you to see the gaps in your students' writing, and to look for both positive and negative trends. This will assist you in planning individual conferences and whole-group mini-lessons.

No matter how you go about recording your students' progress, make sure that the information you gather can be used to drive future instruction. We have included examples of recording sheets on the next two pages. Adapt them to make recording a tool that will enhance—not hinder—your teaching.

Writer's Workshop-Conference Form

Name_____ Topic_____ + − date_____	Name_____ Topic_____ + − date_____	Name_____ Topic_____ + − date_____
Name_____ Topic_____ + − date_____	Name_____ Topic_____ + − date_____	Name_____ Topic_____ + − date_____
Name_____ Topic_____ + − date_____	Name_____ Topic_____ + − date_____	Name_____ Topic_____ + − date_____
Name_____ Topic_____ + − date_____	Name_____ Topic_____ + − date_____	Name_____ Topic_____ + − date_____

Mini-lesson needs

Writing Observations

Name_____

Conference	To Do

Piece_____ _____
Piece_____ _____
Piece_____ _____

Piece_____ _____
Piece_____ _____
Piece_____ _____

Piece_____ _____
Piece_____ _____
Piece_____ _____

Piece_____ _____
Piece_____ _____
Piece_____ _____

Piece_____ _____
Piece_____ _____
Piece_____ _____

Piece_____ _____
Piece_____ _____
Piece_____ _____

Piece_____ _____
Piece_____ _____
Piece_____ _____

Piece_____ _____
Piece_____ _____
Piece_____ _____

Piece_____ _____
Piece_____ _____
Piece_____ _____

Growing Up Writing: Mini-Lessons for Emergent and Beginning Writers
© 2003, Connie Campbell Dierking and Sherra Ann Jones, Maupin House Publishing

Part Three: Sharing

Sharing is the third and final part of writer's workshop. After direct instruction and independent practice, it is time for students to share their writing with the whole group.

Your writing community should provide feedback to every member. It assists the author in identifying what is working in his piece. It also inspires revision. Feedback should be positive, constructive, and honest. It will need to be modeled many, many times before your young students internalize what it looks like and sounds like. Be patient, and it will come.

Sharing begins with a signal to return to the common area where the workshop began. Some teachers use music, some a hand signal, some a light switch. Whatever you choose, make sure the class understands that the signal means "return to the common area, now." As with expectations for behavior during silent/quiet writing, make students understand that returning to the common area quickly is not negotiable. This makes for a smooth transition.

This portion of workshop should take no longer than fifteen minutes. Having a process for who will share and when is imperative. Whatever your process—pulling names out of jar, choosing a table a day, child of the day, etc.—your students must understand and follow it. If they don't, you will be bombarded by "Can I share? Can I share?" Our process is described in Operational Mini-Lesson 3.

Author's Chair

Have a special spot for authors to sit in while they share. They should sit in this spot and read their piece clearly to the class. Mini-lessons on speaking loudly, holding their papers, and sharing illustrations will make this time more effective.

Feedback: Notices, Questions, and Reminders

We teach our students how to respond to their peers' writing by modeling three types of feedback. The first type requires them to state something they noticed or liked about the author's piece. This might sound like "I noticed that your bike is blue" or "I liked that you left spaces between your words." A polite "thank you" is the author's response. **Notices** help the author recognize strengths or weaknesses in their piece. We allow three students to give a notice.

The second type of feedback invites questions. For example, "How old were you when you learned to ride your bike?" or "Do you have any other brothers or sisters?" The author responds by answering the questions. **Questions** help the author consider details and focus for revision. Three students ask a question about the piece.

The third type of feedback is **reminders**. Here students listen for a connection to their own life. This might sound like "When you said you had a blue bike that reminded me of my bike. It's blue, too." Only one or two students are allowed to give reminders, because most children will probably have a story they'd like to share. That's the power of this form of feedback: encourage your students to use un-shared reminders as a topic in their own piece on another writing day.

Backdoor Teaching during Sharing

Backdoor teaching allows the teacher to make teaching points on the go. These points were not the focus of the mini-lessons but present themselves for quick authentic instruction. Because the entire class has heard the same piece, you are able to provide specific feedback that benefits not only the author, but also the entire class. For example, "I noticed that you had a hard time re-reading your piece. What would make re-reading easier next time?" The discussion that follows might include leaving spaces, providing more letter/sound correspondence, or writing from left to right. All these ideas will enable the audience—as well as the author— to examine their writing practice. This is a very powerful use of sharing time.

What Expectations Should I Have for Writer's Workshop?

Because of the daily opportunity to practice their writing skills, your students will begin to view the world through the eyes of a writer. They will look forward to writing during workshop time. A dove returning to her nest in the gutter above the garage becomes a writing topic. Passing an ambulance on the way to school, a rock collection, or a scored goal are experiences intentionally stored as writing topics. Children who are given time to write every day will learn to value the small moments in their lives and look forward to recording them.

In short, you can expect your students to become better, more observant writers.

Publishing

As noted, publishing is not the goal of our writing curriculum. But throughout the year, we do work some pieces through all the steps of the writing process.

Publishing in kindergarten can look like a handwritten book with illustrations or a type-written sheet of paper. It may be a poster or a card. Keep it simple. Not every piece taken through the writing process has to be bound in a book. Invite the principal in to hear sharing time. Record stories on cassette tape to be shared at home. Send your young authors to the media specialist, custodian, or another class to read their pieces. Making publication public validates the importance of completing the writing process. Celebrate the writing, not just the published work.

How Do I Find Time to Incorporate Writer's Workshop into My Day?

First, recognize that the teaching of writing can be incorporated with and supported by all curriculum areas. While your students are engaged in writer's workshop, they are not only practicing writing, they are practicing reading, spelling, grammar, and handwriting. The application of these skills are applied directly when student's write.

Mini-lessons can be connected to any given unit of study. If you are learning about weather in science, your mini-lesson in writer's workshop could be ways to use a diagram of clouds to support a piece of writing. Within a unit on patriotism, writing mini-lessons can reflect the importance of character development, sequencing, or elaboration.

Rethink your current daily schedule. Activities that we have always done "just because" need to be reexamined for importance. We realized several years ago that a string of morning jobs for children to complete as they entered the room was random and not meeting the needs of our students. Once we recognized that, we restructured our day to begin with independent reading. Twenty new minutes were added to our schedule for distribution throughout the day. Below is our new daily schedule. This is what works for us.

Daily Kindergarten Schedule

8:00-8:20: Announcements/Independent Reading
8:20-8:30: Word of the Day
8:30-9:30: Writer's Workshop
- Mini-Lesson
- Independent Practice/Conferencing
- Sharing
9:30-10:00: Outside Play
- Gross Motor Activities
10:00-11:00: Reader's Workshop
- Mini-lesson
  - Shared Reading
  - Read aloud
  - Interactive Charts
- Independent and Guided Practice
  - Centers
  - Book Baskets
  - Guided Reading
- Sharing
  - Individual responses
11:00-11:30: Lunch
11:30-12:00: Rest
12:00-12:30: Math
12:30-1:00: Specials
- P.E.
- Music
- Art
- Guidance
1:00-1:45: Centers (content integrated with workshop activities)
1:45-1:55: Interactive Writing
2:00: Dismiss

Seven Keys for a Successful Writer's Workshop

1. Writer's workshop needs to be a daily part of your schedule.

2. Intentional reading/writing connections should be embraced.

3. All three parts (mini-lesson, independent practice with conferencing, and sharing) need to be in place for every workshop.

4. The writing process should be defined. Expect that students will have pieces in various stages of the writing process. Most pieces will not be published.

5. The teacher must model writing often and throughout the day.

6. All students need the opportunity to conference with the teacher at least once a week.

7. All students need to feel their classroom is a safe environment for sharing their writing.

CHAPTER THREE

The Mini-Lesson

Writer's workshop begins with the ritual of a mini-lesson. This is a time for your entire class to gather and discuss writing. It is a predictable beginning to writer's workshop and allows you to address skills the entire class needs to improve their writing.

A mini-lesson is your lesson plan for one day's writing instruction. It should instruct and inspire. Mini-lessons are usually directed towards a target skill. Most last from ten to fifteen minutes. (This can vary widely—how long a particular lesson lasts is determined by the nature of the lesson.) How long the mini-lesson lasts is not as important as the fact that you begin every workshop with a lesson that is targeted to your students' needs.

Be careful that your mini-lessons do not become maxi-lessons. Keep them trimmed and clean. Ask yourself, "What can I show my students that will make them better writers?" Address that specific targeted skill and move on: the bulk of writer's workshop should be spent in the practice of writing, not in the talk leading up to it.

Remember that the mini-lesson is not used to determine what your students will be writing about during their independent practice time. Independent practice is reserved for your students to write freely about whatever they choose. Although we hope that our students will apply the day's mini-lesson to their writing that particular day, it does not always happen. That's okay. During the mini-lesson, you are only showing your students what a particular skill looks like. It is, as Lucy Calkins puts it, "adding ideas to the class pot." Your students will begin to sample what's been stewing in that pot as they become more comfortable with the ingredients and processes of their own writing. Many target skills will need to be repeated in mini-lessons over and over before you'll notice their widespread use in your students' writing.

Mini-lessons might address a target skill that pertains only to a small group of students. That's fine. It's beneficial for all students to hear about a new skill, even though only a few might be able to attempt the application in their writing.

As with the three parts of writer's workshop, following a predictable pattern when presenting a mini-lesson will enhance your students' long-term learning. Mini-lessons should contain four phases that move quickly and seamlessly from one to the next.

The Four Phases of a Mini-Lesson

Connection

Begin every mini-lesson with a connection. Share with your students what you will be teaching them and connect it to their previous learning. This gives the lesson extended purpose. An example might sound like this:

"Yesterday we were talking about how important it is to reread your piece in order to revise and make it better. When you were reading your piece yesterday, many of you noticed you left something out. Today, I am going to show you how to use a symbol to insert information you may have forgotten."

The connection should be brief. You are merely telling them what you will be teaching and how it is related to what they have already learned. This portion of the workshop generally lasts from one to two minutes.

Teach

The next phase is to teach your students something they will use in their writing. Your purpose is to define, model, and demonstrate, with the intent that your students will use the information in their own writing. Use this time for the giving and gathering of information. As you address the skill you are introducing (or reinforcing), make note of your students' reactions. Do they seem engaged or confused? Later, you will use this information during the conferencing stage of writer's workshop.

Make sure you provide models for the skill that you are teaching. You may use your writing, student writing, or published literature as models of instruction.

This portion of the workshop may last anywhere from three to ten minutes, depending on your mode of delivery. Obviously, the use of a piece of literature will require more time. Try to retain your focus. Teach the skill and move on!

Engagement

This is the time for your students to try what you have just taught them. It is most often done orally. This is not their independent practice time. That comes in part two of the workshop cycle.

Engagement may take the form of a group or partner share. The following are examples of oral engagement:

"Turn to your partner and share a describing word."
"Turn to your partner and tell them what you going to write about."
"Share a good title for my story with your partner."

Another way to give children the opportunity to practice is to have them engage in a quick-write. A quick-write is simply an opportunity for all students to attempt the skill in print with group support. For example, if your target skill was writing similes, then a quick-write might be to have everyone write a simile using the color blue. After a few minutes, select a few students to share.

Engagement can last from one to five minutes.

Link

Link the mini-lesson to your students' on-going literacy instruction. A link is a simple reminder that the skill you are teaching has a place in the larger picture of their writing development. It might sound like this:

"Today and every day, remember to leave spaces between words."
"Who is going to try labeling their picture today?"
"Today and every day, I would like you to remember to start all sentences with a capital letter."

A link should be short, explicit, and directed to the whole class. A minute or less is all it takes.

After the link, signal to your students that it is time for them to transition into their independent practice time. See Operational Mini-Lesson 7 on page 52 for hints on managing this transition.

Mini-Lessons Categorized by Function

We have defined four categories of mini-lessons. These categories include operational, print awareness, foundational, and craft mini-lessons. Lessons from each category are essential to a balanced writing program. Although the balance of types will shift throughout the year, it is important to include all four types of lessons in your instruction.

Operational Mini-Lessons

Operational mini-lessons are lessons that define writer's workshop and its procedures. These are the lessons that lay the foundation for the entire school year. Students cannot do their best writing in a classroom where processes have not been defined. Transitioning to the gathering area, where to keep journals, when to sharpen a pencil, etc., are all management techniques that are addressed through operational mini-lessons.

Target Skills: introducing and managing materials, defining writer's workshop, managing time and space, giving and receiving feedback, conferencing etiquette, understanding and using a rubric

Anything that interferes with your teaching needs to be addressed in order for your writing community to function effectively. The mini-lesson format is perfect for defining procedures that will make the workshop process work. It is imperative to include children in the design of these processes in order for ownership to occur. Ownership builds community. In a community, members follow procedures, behave respectfully, and offer support to each other. Procedures must be taught and behaviors continually modeled. Building a community is essential for budding writers to take risks and move forward with their writing.

We use operational mini-lessons for demonstrating how to give and receive feedback. These lessons involve the role playing of appropriate comments and the asking of specific questions. For the most part, these lessons are oral and interactive.

Conferencing etiquette is another skill we address through operational mini-lessons. Conferences can't work if you are plagued with countless interruptions from other students seeking your attention. These lessons teach students to actively listen and respect the purpose of the conference.

Lastly, operational mini-lessons address understanding and using a rubric to assess writing. Rubrics help your students be authentically involved with improving their writing. See Operational Mini-Lessons 15 through 18.

Although operational lessons take place throughout the school year, the heaviest concentration occurs in the first month of school. The first month is when balancing operational lessons with lessons that address writing itself is most difficult. It is hard to resist the desire to move ahead with print awareness, foundation, and craft lessons, but you must spend some time developing your writing procedures to ensure the growth of your writing community. Operational mini-lessons allow processes to be put in place so children can be responsible for their own learning within a writing community.

Print Awareness Mini-Lessons

A basic skill necessary for reading and writing is the understanding that print carries certain conventions. These conventions allow the reader to understand the message of the writer. Isolated drills and worksheets that cover punctuation, spacing, or capital letters provide little transfer to real writing. Allowing students to use these conventions within their own writing empowers them to improve their pieces authentically. Explicit instruction of conventions is covered under the umbrella of print awareness mini-lessons.

Print awareness mini-lessons directly address the reading-writing connection. The skills these lessons address are the foundation for both activities. Writer's workshop will enhance your students' performance in each.

> Target Skills: managing space, spaces between words, left to right, top to bottom, return sweep, letter-sound correspondence, word families, temporary spelling, period, question marks, quotation marks, capital letters

Early in the year the majority of your writing lessons will be comprised of operational and print awareness mini-lessons. As print awareness develops, you will begin to see your students apply their knowledge as they write. Spaces will be apparent between words, sentences will start with capital letters, and temporary spelling will begin to include beginning, middle, and ending sounds. These are indicators that students are becoming communicators through writing.

When you see your students beginning to internalize print awareness skills, it will be time for a shift in the focus of your mini-lessons. Look to foundational and craft mini-lessons to help hone your students' skills.

Foundational Mini-Lessons

Foundational mini-lessons are the building blocks of good writing. These are lessons that will assist with the basic organization of a piece. Students will carry these strategies with them throughout every genre and every stage of the writing process. A writer may change or modify her style, but the foundations of her writing skill will remain constant. Think of foundational mini-lessons as the foundation of a house.

Target Skills: choosing a topic, beginning, middle and end, leads, endings, focus, transition words, setting, character development, sequencing, titles

Choosing a topic is one foundational skill that we practice through mini-lessons. We use children's literature, student examples, photographs, etc., to inspire and instruct. Any book that connects to the life of a kindergartner could be the basis for a mini-lesson on topic selection. A mini-lesson using a shared story about a bug can remind other students about their own insect tales. Bring in interesting photos or objects to inspire topics.

After selecting topics, foundational mini-lessons will also assist students in the sequencing of their thoughts, the effectiveness of a powerful lead and ending, beginnings, middles, and endings, and the use of transition words to help their pieces flow.

Foundational mini-lessons occur throughout the year as students develop as proficient writers. They also lay the framework for craft mini-lessons. Once students have strategies for getting their ideas on paper, craft mini-lessons have more meaning and can be integrated.

Craft Mini-Lessons

Target Skills: details, active verbs, alliteration, elaboration, similes, comparing/contrasting, description and moving from general to specific, varied sentences

"Crafted places in texts are those places where writers do particular things with words that go beyond just choosing the ones they need to get the meaning across."

—Katie Wood Ray, *Wondrous Words*

Craft mini-lessons are considerations to move writing beyond basic proficiency. The manipulation and choice of words and structures are the basis for these types of mini-lessons.

As kindergarten writers build a foundation and begin using strategies to compose complete thoughts it is time to consider integrating craft mini-lessons into your instructional strategies. Craft lessons teach children how to manipulate their writing to make it better. The word "craft" implies a special way of doing something. Showing young writers they have choices in the words and designs of their pieces will open up a new writing world. A sentence that could read "I love my mom" becomes "I love my mom as much as a flower loves the rain."

Craft mini-lessons can be interactive and diverse. During craft lessons, the class should be actively involved in doing something that will improve their writing pieces. Role-playing allows students to witness the difference between "I went to the playground" and "I skipped to the playground." Standing on a stool and shouting, "I am the king of the world!" sounds very different than whispering, "I am the king of the world." Showing children how interchanging shouting and whispering paints a different picture in that one sentence.

Preparing a treat together and then reconstructing the event using specific verbs will allow students to hear good word choice. Kneading dough to make homemade bread is a specific action. Using the word "knead" in a piece about making bread is more specific than "mix." Showing children the difference while actively engaged in the process is powerful. The essence of a craft lesson is showing not telling.

Content area pieces are a good place to practice craft lessons. Showing students how to compose one compare and contrast piece from two separate pieces about a butterfly and a moth would be a craft lesson that integrates science. Description is an important skill in science, math, and social studies. Practicing oral and written description during writer's workshop will allow this skill to permeate other subject areas. Using attributes to describe shape, depiction of a specific period of history, or characteristics of a marine animal all lend themselves to authentic practice in description.

Let your favorite authors become your co-teachers in writing. Look at the picture books in your classrooms. There are thousands of craft lessons found in literature books. Which books have great examples of elaboration, varied sentences, or the use of details? Put those books aside to use as examples during a craft lesson. Teach your students to read as writers. If one of their favorite picture books uses beautiful similes then encourage them to try a simile in their own writing. Teach them to listen for writer-ly moves that they admire. Discuss what the author did and then show them what it might look like in their own writing. The literature list on page 127 will assist you in choosing books to address specific target skills.

Craft mini-lessons are lessons that elevate writing. They are an integral part of the revision process, and should be taught in kindergarten even if you are not having your students move their pieces through the entire writing process.

Common Questions Concerning Mini-Lessons

How will I know which mini-lesson to teach?

Knowing your students well is the essence of knowing which lesson to teach, and when. It is also important to know your district and state expectations in writing. These expectations will identify target skills and give you specifics in making writing goals for your students. Your district's goals should guide your instruction.

Where do mini-lessons come from?

District expectations

Determine the skills that you should target by examining your district's writing expectations. These may include letter/sounds correspondence, focus, description, etc.

Students

No one knows your students better than you do. What do you notice in day-to-day writing? Look for gaps or trends. Address these areas in mini-lessons. If most of your students are writing multiple sentences, it may be time to teach them how to add specific details. Celebrate the positives and provide models and demonstrations for areas of need. Ask permission to use a student's actual writing piece to share with the class. Give feedback to one student publicly and the rest of the class will benefit. Use writings from previous years and from other grade levels. Allow students to help each other.

Your Own Writing

Many teachers are afraid of their own writing! Please don't be! So you're not a Cynthia Rylant or a Jane Yolen—you still have something to give to your community of writers. From time to time, share a piece of your writing and ask the class for suggestions. Compose on an easel in front of the class, thinking aloud as you write. Share your questions and decisions as you work through the piece. Express delight in sentences that work well and tell your students why. At the kindergarten level, simple sentences and lists can lead to extended pieces. Model this in front of your students, demonstrating how you turn a simple sentence such as "I like my cat" into a paragraph. Portray yourself as a learner in the workshop. Children need to know that the teacher doesn't always have all the answers and that we struggle in our writing as well. Being a part of a writing community demands that we are participants. Using your own writing as a resource for mini-lessons is a necessary activity for belonging to the group.

Literature

Children's literature provides a springboard to teach most any writing skill. Through literature students are able to see and hear quality writing. These authors are the masters of words and can provide models in every genre. However, a word of caution: when using literature students must first hear the book in its entirety. The author wrote the book to convey a message. Hearing the book piecemeal would do disservice to the reader and the listener. Once a class has enjoyed a book for the story, it can be used as a tool for instruction. Examining specific writing traits and techniques in literature make powerful mini-lessons.

Should there be a balance among different types of mini-lessons?

Yes, there should be a balance between different types of mini-lessons. You would be wasting your time trying to teach a lot of foundational and craft lessons before processes are in place for managing materials, time, and behavior during writer's workshop, so at the beginning of the year we do many operational and print awareness lessons. As the school year progresses, you will begin to teach more foundational and craft lessons.

Will I need to teach a mini-lesson more than once?

Yes, there will be times when you will need to teach a string of mini-lessons on the same target skill. Most often students do not internalize a skill the first time it is introduced.

Thinking about your lessons in units of study is helpful in re-teaching a target skill. For example, a unit of study on revision will allow a week's worth of lessons on adding details to a piece of writing. Another example would be a unit of study on leads. You could teach a string of mini-lessons on various types of leads using literature, student writing, and your own compositions. However, even after a string of mini-lessons, target skills may have to be revisited!

What about publishing?

You should have your students move some of their pieces through all the steps of the writing process, including revisions and publishing. But publishing does not have to be the goal of your writing program. The majority of your students' pieces will be more valuable as models of instruction and as opportunities for authentic practice.

In which genres are kindergartners most comfortable?

Begin with expository genres such as personal narrative or descriptive writing. As Marcia Freeman notes, expository writing is the natural medium of emergent writers who are always striving to describe or explain their world. Expository genres (which teach kindergartners how to explain, describe, or inform) tend to engage the young writer.

Interestingly, while kindergartners love to tell narratives, they seem to gravitate away from fiction in our workshops.

What happens when a small percentage of the class is not ready to move on?

It is not a mystery that students learn at different rates, and that the task of meeting individual needs is difficult. Small-group instruction is an essential component of workshop. Small group can happen during the quiet-writing portion of writer's workshop. Pulling a homogeneous group that requires remediation on a specific skill or strategy allows the rest of the class to practice within their zone of proximal development while you are able to give the small group the added support that they need.

Small-group instruction can be supplemented by peer tutoring. For example, pair a student who is having difficulty leaving spaces between words with a peer. Encourage them to have conversation regarding spaces. The student who has mastered this skill can verbalize strategies and assist her friend in doing the same. With the added support of a peer, mastery may occur.

Shared teaching is another suggestion for meeting the needs of students. Grouping students homogeneously for a short period of time will allow you to focus your instruction on specific needs of the group. We suggest dividing students into three groups based on writing mastery. When we implemented this strategy our groups consisted of a group that was not meeting district expectations, a group working on grade level, and a group that was working above grade level. We developed a specific lesson plan to ensure students were being instructed at their level. For example, the lower group worked specifically on segmenting sounds. The middle group practiced using details in sentences, and the top group engaged in writing paragraphs. The intervention lasted for two weeks.

Are students required to try the mini-lesson?

No. Regardless of their abilities, students should not be required to apply the mini-lesson during independent writing time. Some students may not be developmentally ready for the skill. They may attempt the skill at a later date when they are ready or after subsequent mini-lessons on the same skill have been presented. Other students may be in the middle of a piece that is not conducive to the lesson that was presented.

However, if the majority of your students are ready for a mini-lesson on elaboration, don't be afraid to present that lesson to the whole class. The students who are ready for elaboration will hopefully choose to apply it in their current writing. The students who are not ready to apply the skill still need to hear what elaboration sounds like. All students benefit from all mini-lessons regardless of their writing development. Specific individual needs will be met through conferencing and small group instruction.

Should I teach a mini-lesson every day?

Yes, there should be some type of direct instruction specific to writing every day. Some lessons may be operational and only take a few minutes. Others may be more involved. The predictable structure of writer's workshop allows for a mini-lesson daily. The children will come to expect this as a part of their writing routine.

Should students always write independently after a mini-lesson?

Yes. After the mini-lesson, students should always write independently. Even if your mini-lesson is operational, students need to move to the second part of writer's workshop, independent writing. Because students have their own journals and are responsible for choosing a writing topic, they are able to write independently after any type of mini-lesson.

A Top Ten List for Effective Mini-Lessons

1. Use your students' needs and your district's expectations to determine mini-lessons.

2. Keep mini-lessons as short as possible.

3. Stay focused on your goal for the lesson.

4. Use student writing for mini-lessons.

5. Children's literature provides excellent models. Use it.

6. Don't be afraid to repeat a mini-lesson over a few days.

7. When you develop charts during mini-lessons, post them in the classroom as reminders.

8. Occasionally write in front of your students.

9. Keep track of your mini-lessons.

10. Not every child is going to "get it" and that's okay!

CHAPTER FOUR

A Year at a Glance

We start writer's workshop on the first day of school. Our expectation is that everyone will participate. We use the first month to begin building our writing community. Even though every child will not understand how print is oriented on the page, they are all eager to engage in the behavior of writing. We accept all approximations and encourage our young writers to take risks. Our instruction is focused on operations related to the workshop routine. We also give attention to the concepts of print and letter-sound correspondence.

By the middle of the year, student writing demonstrates print concepts. Left to right orientation, correct return sweep, and spaces between words are evident. You will see phonetically related approximations and some sight words spelled correctly. Students should be able to express at least one complete thought that can be read with little translation from the student. Instructional focus moves to the development of a simple sentence that makes sense. Children practice strategies for correctly spelling simple sight words and approximating more challenging words. Conventions are modeled.

Towards the end of the year, students are writing sentences with specific details. Simple sight words are spelled correctly and there are enough phonemes in words for writing to be easily translated. Capital letters are used at the beginning of sentences and some punctuation is evident. Students engage in writing pieces that have a simple beginning, middle, and end. You will see students attempting to craft their writing. Instruction now consists of more foundational and craft mini-lessons than operational and print awareness.

Included on the following pages are a chart of benchmarked skills for writing instruction in the kindergarten year, a calendar of mini-lessons for days 1 through 20, and a calendar of mini-lessons for days 90 through 109. We chose these days for these calendars to assist you in beginning your year and to benchmark mid-year expectations. These progressions have worked for us.

You will notice that the first month includes nine operational mini-lessons and six print awareness mini-lessons, but only three foundational mini-lessons and two craft mini-lessons. As stated earlier, the beginning of the school year demands many operational and print awareness mini-lessons. As you move beyond the first month, operational mini-lessons will become less important. However, there will be times when you will need to revisit or tweak a process. The focus of print awareness lessons will move away from the orientation of print towards letter/sound correspondence.

On the first day of school, we begin with a foundational mini-lesson. We want the children to have a positive experience with writing before the heavy concentration on workshop operations. It also gives us a writing piece we can use for assessing each child's current writing abilities.

The mid-year calendar only has three operational mini-lessons and three print awareness mini-lessons, but ten foundational and four craft mini-lessons. Notice how the balance has shifted.

You will see follow-up lessons noted on the mini-lesson calendars. This indicates that the original lesson has already been taught. The follow-up provides extra support in mastery of a target skill.

We realize that teachers operate under the guidelines of their own district and state expectations. We also realize that many variables affect instructional decisions, such as class size, student abilities, and teaching styles. You may find it necessary to change the order of our lessons or stretch one lesson into a few days. Do what works best for you.

Our pacing is based on a belief that writer's workshop happens every day. Because our students write every day, they leave kindergarten exceeding expectations. Yours will too.

Benchmarks for Writing Skills by Month

August

- follows a routine for writer's workshop
- understands that print carries a message
- draws a picture
- tells details about a picture
- uses mock letters or random strings of letters
- generates ideas to write about

September

- knows the difference between a letter and a word
- identifies a vowel and a consonant
- practices segmenting sounds
- labels pictures with some beginning sounds

October

- leaves spaces between words
- writes from left to right, top to bottom
- writes to express one thought
- writes a list
- uses many beginning sounds

November

- spells some sight words correctly
- print begins to match picture
- begins to use ending sounds
- uses temporary spelling
- uses a rubric to score writing

December

- uses close spelling approximations of simple words
- one complete thought can be read without student translation
- uses some capital letters
- uses some punctuation
- uses consistent spacing
- writes a simple letter

January

- uses close spelling approximations of more challenging words
- begins to show evidence of organization
- uses at least one detail word in a sentence
- sentences make sense
- develops a plan for improving writing
- uses some revision strategies

February

- simple sight words are spelled correctly
- uses some medial vowel sounds
- uses a logical sequence of ideas
- uses specific word choice

March

- uses pronouns
- begins to identify focus
- uses a lead sentence
- uses a simile appropriately

April

- titles a piece
- use capital letters correctly
- writes only complete thoughts

May

- develops beginning and ending
- correct punctuation evident
- uses strategies to correctly spell words
- uses specific details

Growing Up Writing: Mini-Lessons for Emergent and Beginning Writers
© 2003, Connie Campbell Dierking and Sherra Ann Jones, Maupin House Publishing

Sample First Month Writing Plans
A Balanced Approach

Day One Writing as Communication **Foundational Mini-Lesson 1**	**Day Two** Guided Drawing / Segmentation **Print Awareness Mini-Lesson 13**	**Day Three** Introducing the First Journal **Operational Mini-Lesson 1**	**Day Four** Defining Writer's Workshop **Operational Mini-Lesson 2**	**Day Five** Process for Sharing **Operational Mini-Lesson 3**
Day Six Temporary Spelling **Print Awareness Mini-Lesson 1**	**Day Seven** Managing Journals **Operational Mini-Lesson 4**	**Day Eight** Managing Writing Tools **Operational Mini-Lesson 5**	**Day Nine** Every Sound Needs a Letter **Print Awareness Mini-Lesson 2**	**Day Ten** Practicing Transitions **Operational Mini-Lesson 7**
Day Eleven Letters Make Words **Print Awareness Mini-Lesson 3**	**Day Twelve** Spaces Between Words **Print Awareness Mini-Lesson 4**	**Day Thirteen** Generating Ideas to Write About **Foundational Mini-Lesson 2**	**Day Fourteen** Using Details in Writing **Craft Mini-Lesson 1**	**Day Fifteen** Feedback **Operational Mini-Lesson 8**
Day Sixteen Audience Ettiquette **Operational Mini-Lesson 9**	**Day Seventeen** Making a Brainstorm List **Foundational Mini-Lesson 3**	**Day Eighteen** Color Words **Craft Mini-Lesson 3**	**Day Nineteen** Managing Space **Print Awareness Mini-Lesson 4**	**Day Twenty** Conference Etiquette **Operational Mini-Lesson 10**

Sample Fifth Month Writing Plans
A Balanced Approach

Day Ninety Using Literature to Generate Topics **Foundational Mini-Lesson 4**	**Day Ninety-one** Using Literature to Generate Topics **Foundational Mini-Lesson 4 Follow-Up**	**Day Ninety-two** Using Literature to Generate Topics **Foundational Mini-Lesson 4 Follow-Up**	**Day Ninety-three** Using Literature to Generate Topics **Foundational Mini-Lesson 4 Follow-Up**	**Day Ninety-four** Using Literature to Generate Topics **Foundational Mini-Lesson 4 Follow-Up**
Day Ninety-five Adding On To Previous Writing **Operational Mini-Lesson 14**	**Day Ninety-six** Temporary or Invented Spelling **Print Awareness Mini-Lesson 1 Follow-Up**	**Day Ninety-seven** Every Sound Needs a Letter **Print Awareness Mini-Lesson 2 Follow-Up**	**Day Ninety-eight** Active Verbs **Craft Mini-Lesson 2**	**Day Ninety-nine** Description **Foundational Mini-Lesson 5**
Day One Hundred Words Have Families **Print Awareness Mini-Lesson 10**	**Day One Hundred One** Assessing Writing Using a Rubric **Operational Mini-Lesson 17**	**Day One Hundred Two** Making a Plan for Improving Writing **Operational Mini-Lesson 18**	**Day One Hundred Three** Sequencing Information **Foundational Mini-Lesson 7**	**Day One Hundred Four** Using Transition Words **Foundational Mini-Lesson 11**
Day One Hundred Five Beginning, Middle, End **Foundational Mini-Lesson 12**	**Day One Hundred Six** Connecting Sentences Using 'And' **Craft Mini-Lesson 6**	**Day One Hundred Seven** Inserting Information **Craft Mini-Lesson 12**	**Day One Hundred Eight** Leads **Foundational Mini-Lesson 6 Follow-Up**	**Day One Hundred Nine** Specific Word Choice **Craft Mini-Lesson 9**

CHAPTER FIVE

Connecting to Parents

Most parents are interested in the types of literacy instruction that take place in their child's classroom. Many want to help their budding writers and readers, but aren't sure how. If you give them some strategies for helping their child, they will be happy to give you added support. In fact, parental involvement will be essential to your success.

At the kindergarten level, parents often think of writing instruction only as handwriting practice. They don't see the connection between writing and reading instruction. You will need to give them direction. This might take the form of a newsletter, a parent workshop, or a menu of specific ideas. However you do it, make sure you do it. Including parents in the development of your writing community will make them more comfortable when enjoying the content of their children's writing.

We invite parents into our classrooms. Some prefer night workshops on writing development, while others choose to visit our classrooms during the school day to see a writer's workshop in action. We share our writing rubrics and give them examples of the different stages. We educate them about temporary spelling so they are aware that their children must feel free to take risks in their writing. We share the devastation that can occur if children are forced to only write words they can spell. Parents understand that creative juices do not flow if constrained by correct spelling. (We continually assure them that spelling does have a place in our classrooms, just not in the first drafts of emergent writers.)

Writing is a part of our weekly homework. Family writing ideas are placed in the class newsletter so parents can enjoy writing with their children at home. Specific writing ideas are shared at conferences and during PTA meetings. Talking writing with our parents is almost as common as it is with our students.

Finally, parents are invited to school twice a year to hear readings of our students' published pieces. These are pieces that have been taken completely through the writing process. Students occupy the author's chair and celebrate their writing accomplishments.

This chapter assembles ideas we have used to connect with our students' parents. Some could be adapted and used with volunteers in the classroom. Some are simply explanations of activities that could be used in journals for homework. Most activities are reinforcements of mini-lessons from the daily writer's workshop.

Writing Questionnaire

At the beginning of the school year, we find it interesting to get to know our students as writers. We send home a questionnaire that each student fills out with their parents' help. As a class, we review the information. We are able to begin building our writing community by recognizing writing rituals that we have in common. You may find your class prefers writing with pens. This is information you can use when making determinations about writing tool procedures.

When developing any classroom procedure, always consider Best Practices and your own comfort zone. For example, even though your students may have voiced a preference for writing on the floor, you may not feel comfortable with your students spread out and using clipboards. Explain your feelings to your students and offer to try it at a later date.

Although you are ultimately responsible for management and instructional decisions, keep in mind that children respond best when they have ownership. A questionnaire that is examined and then considered by the whole class will build community within the system. A reproducible example is included on the next page.

A Writing Questionnaire

1. Would you rather write

__at a desk at school

__on the floor

__outside under a tree

__in your bedroom

2. Would you rather be writing

__a recipe

__a make-believe story

__a how-to story

__a poem

3. Would you rather write on

__lined paper

__unlined paper

__chart paper

__stapled together paper

4. Would you rather write with

__a pencil

__a marker

__crayons

__a pen

5. Would you rather share your piece with

__a friend

__a teacher

__a family member

__the principal

Reflective Writing Homework

Reflective writing is an activity that gives students an opportunity to engage in free-writing at home, where parents can observe their child practicing writing behaviors. During reflective writing, students are simply given a notebook or journal and are encouraged to write about any topic for ten minutes. Often this free-writing time will lead to a writing topic during writer's workshop the next day.

The intent of the assignment is for students to get their thoughts and ideas down on paper. When explaining the assignment to parents, remind them that this is not the time to be concerned about correct spelling. Parents are encouraged to respond positively to the content of their child's writing, and to accept all approximate spellings. It is also important for children to share their writing orally with their parents.

For this activity, we use small spiral notebooks, or we simply staple sheets of paper together to make a small book. The children take these home on the night of reflective-writing homework and return them the next day.

We introduce reflective-writing homework after the winter break. Once students and parents are introduced to the routine, we send it home about once a week.

How you respond to the reflective journals is up to you. We have done it in several ways. Sometimes we make a written comment about the entry. Other times we simply put a sticker at the bottom of the page. Buddy-sharing is another way to acknowledge the writing. There is no right or wrong way to respond. Always remember, however, that children write best when they are addressing a specific audience.

On the first night of reflective-writing homework we staple a letter of explanation to a journal. This letter outlines the expectations and the process. A reproducible example is included on the next page.

Dear Parents,

Tonight is the first night of reflective writing homework. Reflective writing is an activity that gives your child an opportunity to engage in writing at home, where you can observe your young author practicing writing behaviors. Reflective writing also gives your child a chance to write about something that matters to him.

You will give your child ten minutes of uninterrupted time to write about any topic. Encourage him to write about anything that he wants to. If your child is reluctant or has difficulty getting started, there are many ways to prompt him.

One good way to get started is to read a favorite book. Talk with your child about the story. Have your child share a favorite character or a funny event. Then ask your child to record those thoughts in the reflective writing journal.

Another idea is to have a simple conversation. For example, talk about favorites. Encourage your young writer to tell you about their favorite toy, food, activity, or animal. Then have him record his thoughts. Talking with your child first will help set a purpose for writing.

Lists are easy to make and are popular with emergent writers. Allow them to make lists of any topic of choice. Colors, fruits, animals, candies, friends, etc. provide list ideas that give your child practice in segmenting sounds and writing words.

Some Important Dos and Don'ts

- ✓ Some children do not need any assistance choosing a writing topic. That is great! Leave them alone and let them write.

- ✓ This is not a time to spell words for your child. Celebrate any attempts to use letter/sound correspondence. Do not correct punctuation.

- ✓ Have your child read their entry to you. Respond positively to the content. Share something you liked about their writing. If you want, ask them a question.

- ✓ When your young writer is ready to begin writing, set a timer for ten minutes. Walk away and allow him or her to write quietly. Listen to the entry after the ten minutes have passed.

- ✓ Send the journal back to school tomorrow.

Thank you for your help with this special homework.

Sincerely,

Writing Practice Menu

The following activities are ideas for writing practice. Although they are addressed to the young student, they are intended to be done with an adult participant. These activities can be used for homework or sent home to extend mini-lessons. You could place them in a brochure to hand out at parent meetings. Offer them as part of a menu of activities that volunteers can conduct while in your classroom. Use these activities in any way that will elevate your writing program.

1. Make an accordion book. Draw a member of your family on each page. Write a few words to describe each person.

2. Choose a stuffed animal. Take it everywhere you go for one day. Record everything you and your animal did that day.

3. Make a peanut butter sandwich. When you are done, write the directions so that someone else in your family can make one. Remember to use transition words like "first," "second," "next," and "finally."

4. Pretend you have one hundred dollars to spend. Look in a catalog. Cut out all the things you would buy. Underneath the picture record what you would do with each item.

5. Design a new bedroom using pictures from a catalog. When you are finished, write about your new room.

6. Choose one place you would like to go. An example might be the beach, the park, or Disney World. Write a letter to your parents telling them all the reasons why they should take you there.

7. Read *Alexander and the No Good, Horrible, Very Bad Day* by Judith Viorst. Think of a very bad day you have had and list all the things that happened to you to make your day no good, horrible, and very bad. Repeat the activity to write about a very good day.

8. Make a simile book that describes you. Similes are comparisons between two objects using the words "like" or "as." An example would be "I'm as quiet as a mouse" or "I'm as brave as a lion."

9. Use your name in a tongue twister. Use members of your family's names in a tongue twister.

10. Think of as many words as you can that mean the same thing as "said," "good," "fun," or "went." Make your own thesaurus.

11. Make an ABC poem using a word for each letter of the alphabet. An example would be "All bubbles can dance easily."

12. Choose a subject you know a lot about. It could be soccer, swimming, riding your bike, or Beanie Babies. Make a list of everything you know about that topic.

13. Write a paragraph about something that is your favorite. It might be your

favorite food, game, treat, season, etc. This is your big idea. Give the reason why that item is your favorite. This is your supporting idea. Write some details about your favorite thing.

Here is an example:

"My favorite treat is ice cream. The reason I like ice cream is because it comes in so many different flavors. When I stand in front of the ice cream counter it is so hard to make a decision. Although I usually choose chocolate chip I know that any flavor would be delicious. I can always count on chocolate chip tasting yummy and sweet. The little chocolate chips in every bite are what make it my favorite. Ice cream is the best treat ever!"

14. Make an inventory of everything in your room.

15. Have a grown-up write a simple sentence on a sheet of paper. An example might be "The boy ran." Take turns adding details to make your sentence grow.

16. Practice writing leads that pull your reader into your piece. Use one of these four types:

   • Write a question. Ask your readers a question or ask yourself one.
     For example: Do you like to go to the beach?
   • Give a hint. Give the readers clear hints or clues as to what your story is about.
     For example: The beach is my favorite place.
   • Provide a sound word.
     For example: Splish, splash, here come the waves.
   • Describe how you feel about the topic.
     For example: I love to go to the beach.

17. Have an adult look for examples of their writing that they can share with you. They could share items they had to write for their job, a letter they wrote, or a grocery list. Ask them to explain how they used words to communicate.

18. Start a dialogue journal with your parents. Write a question for them to answer. Have them answer it and write one for you.

Sending Journals Home

Since they will be writing nearly every day, your students will regularly "finish" a journal by filling in all the pages. They will be proud of these collections of their work, and they will be eager to share their journals with their families.

We like to introduce parents to their child's journals by sending home a version of the following letter with the year's first completed journal. Depending on the level of contact that you've had with parents throughout the beginning of the school year, you might have much to explain about emergent literacy. Remind parents of the importance of temporary spelling. Encourage them to have their children read their journal to them. Make sure they know to praise their child's efforts.

Here's an example of the letter that we use. Use it as a model or feel free to reproduce it.

Dear Parents,

This journal contains your child's first collection of writing. The writing may not be readable to you, but it has meaning for your child.

All children progress developmentally through different stages of writing. This is a process of development that every child must move through at their own pace.

First, they scribble randomly. They may make mock or pretend letters, sometimes stringing them together to resemble words. As their skills grow, children begin to write the letters of the alphabet and use letter sounds to attempt simple words. Eventually they put words together to form sentences.

Young writers understand many more words than they can spell. We want to encourage them to use words in their writing pieces even if they don't know how to spell them correctly. If children are required to write using only words they know how to spell, their writing is limited. I encourage every child to take risks and not be afraid of spelling or punctuation mistakes.

First writing attempts usually only include a few letters that stand for words. This is called "temporary spelling" or "spelling approximations." You may notice examples of temporary spelling in this journal. Celebrate these approximations.

You may find only pictures in this first journal. Pictures can tell many stories and are encouraged. Look for beginning sounds or labels to match the pictures. For example, a picture of a rainbow may be accompanied by the letter "r" or the letters "rabo." These are examples of emergent writing.

Please listen as your child reads or tells you about his journal entries. It may be difficult for them to remember what they wrote. This is common in early writers. As his letter/sound correspondence develops, it will become easier for him to read his writing.

The children in my class practice writing every day. They will consume many journals throughout the year. These will be sent home at the end of each month for you to enjoy.

I look forward to meeting with you during our conference to go over the developmental stages of writing. In the meantime, I hope you enjoy seeing the hard work your young student has been doing.

Sincerely,

Operational Mini-Lessons

Target Skills Addressed

- introducing and managing materials
- defining writer's workshop
- managing time and classroom space
- giving and receiving feedback
- conferencing etiquette
- understanding and using a rubric

Introducing the First Journal

Materials: journals for each student, chart paper, pencils or crayons

Prep Step: Make journals for each student by folding 10 sheets of blank paper into a book. Number the pages from 1-20 on the bottom right corner of the front side only, and add a construction paper cover. Place a red sticker at the top left of the first page of each journal, a yellow sticker at the top left of the second page of each journal, and a blue sticker at the top left of the third page of each journal.

Note: The color of the stickers you put in the journals is only significant in as much as they are the same colors in the same sequence for each student.

Procedure

Explain to your students that today they will be receiving a journal to write in every day during writer's workshop. Show them an example of a journal. Spend time talking about the front of the journal, back of the journal, and the blank pages inside. Be sure to call attention to the numbers at the bottom right. "The first page of your journal is number one, and the last page is number 20. The backs of the pages aren't numbered because we do not write on the back."

Next, show your students the stickers on the first three pages. Explain that the stickers are another clue to help them remember what page to write on the first day, second day, and third day. For example: "Today we will be writing only on page one, the one with the red sticker. Remember, you may not write on the back or move on to page two (with the yellow sticker)." Now pass out the journals. Allow students a few minutes to explore their own books. You may want to conduct a brief review by having students show you the front of their journal, the back of their journal, and page one with the red sticker.

After exploring, show students a journal that has scribbling on the first three pages. Ask them if this is an example of kindergarten writing. Spend

GOAL

To model the appropriate use of a writing journal

time talking about the concept of writing as a form of communication. "People write in order to communicate their thoughts and ideas. A reader would not know what a writer was trying to say just by looking at scribbles." Using chart paper, demonstrate what acceptable journal writing looks like. On the first page you may write the sentence, "I love cats." You would point out how you started at the top left and moved to the right.

Next, you would want to acknowledge that not everyone is ready to write words or sentences. Ask your students if they can think of another way to tell the reader that they like cats. Maybe a picture of them hugging a cat or several cats bordered by hearts would do the trick. They may suggest that you label the picture by writing the name of the cat or the word "love." Some students may only be ready to communicate with pictures or random strings of letters while others may be able to construct a word or sentence using approximations. Regardless of the child's developmental stage, it is important that you model what is acceptable.

Finally, it is time for students to practice writing on the first page of their journal. Before dismissing them to their desks, show them a timer. Explain that you will set the timer for five minutes. They will begin writing when the timer starts, and stop when the timer rings. During writing practice there is to be no talking. You will be walking around the room looking at their work, but they are not to leave their seats. Tell your students that when the timer rings you will give directions for coming back to the gathering spot to share as a community of writers.

Follow Up

Until you have conducted mini-lessons on managing materials, you should be responsible for passing out, collecting, and storing the journals. You will need to continue to reinforce how to use a writing journal appropriately. ■

Defining Writer's Workshop

Materials: student journals, chart paper, pencils or crayons

Prep Step: Produce a copy or overhead of the "Writer's Workshop" graphic from Chapter Two

Procedure

Through a discussion with students, define "workshop" as a place where anything is built using raw materials and tools. You may use the example of a wood workshop. "A carpenter would use materials such as wood, glue, and nails to create a desk or chair. His tools may be a hammer, saw, or screwdriver." Continue the discussion by explaining that in "writer's workshop we will be building our writing skills using a specific process and a variety of materials and tools." Explain that the process has three steps.

> **GOAL**
>
> *To introduce the three steps of writer's workshop*

"The first step is called the mini-lesson. During the mini-lesson we will be gathered together as a community of writers just as we are now. I will present a short lesson that I know will help you to grow as a writer. As a matter of fact, what we are doing now is part of today's mini-lesson." It is wise to remind them of what yesterday's mini-lesson was or what a future lesson might be.

"The second step involves practicing writing. We know that the only way to get better at writing is to write. That's why I will give you time to practice every day.

"The third and last step of writer's workshop is called sharing. After we practice, we will once again gather as a group to share our writing. I will show you how to share your writing and how to listen to others share their writing. You will learn how sharing will help you to grow as a writer even though you will not be the person sharing every day."

As you explain and discuss the three parts of writer's workshop, list them on chart paper so the steps can be displayed and referred to in the future. Before dismissing students to their desks, point out that they are now moving to the practice-writing step of the workshop cycle. Ask if anyone remembers what the class will do after they write.

Follow Up

Until students have internalized the steps of writer's workshop, you will want to continue to refer to the graphic titled "Writer's Workshop" from Chapter Two. It will provide a visual image of the three steps. ■

Writer's Workshop
45 minutes

5 to 10 minutes — 5 to 10 minutes

Sharing
• notice
• question
• personal connect

Mini-Lesson
• connection
• teach
• engage
• link

Independent Practice with Conferencing
• research
• decide
• teach

20 to 30 minutes

A Process to Manage Sharing

Materials: sharing chart

Prep Step: sharing chart (made by gluing one library pocket to a poster board for each child in your class); a craft stick or index card with each child's name on it.

Note: Before presenting this lesson, decide how many children will share per day. We like to have four children share their pieces each day, so our sharing charts consist of six rows of library pockets with four cards in each row. We don't use days of the week to label the rows because sharing occurs consecutively regardless of days off from school. We use differently colored pockets for each row to allow children to visually determine their sharing day.

Procedure

Show the sharing chart to your students. Explain that this chart is going to help them take turns sharing their writing. Point out that there are four pockets in each row, which means that four children will share every day. "We will know whose turn it is to share because a stick or card with their name on it will be in the pocket." Pass out their names and then call one child up at a time to place his name in a pocket. Remind them it does not matter which pocket their name goes in because everyone must take a turn at sharing.

Take a moment to review the steps of writer's workshop with your students. "Today's mini-lesson was my explanation of the sharing chart. What step comes after the mini-lesson? That's right, practice writing comes next. Remember, it is very important for everyone to be quiet during practice writing time. What step comes after we practice? That's right, sharing comes next. That's what we're talking about today—the best way for us to share our writing." Have your students disperse and do their practice writing, then have them re-assemble in the gathering area for sharing.

"These four people (point to row one) will be sharing today. They may choose to share the piece they were working on today, or they may

GOAL

To demonstrate a process for sharing writing

decide to share any piece they are particularly interested in reading." Reiterate that students may not share their writing with the whole class unless it is their turn.

It is also important to make it clear that you reserve the right to change the names in the pockets as you see fit. If someone is absent, you are going to switch their name. Or if a student has implemented a skill or strategy that you know will benefit the group, you may not want to wait for their sharing day. For example, if you presented a mini-lesson on using a left-to-right, top-to-bottom progression and Julie did a great job of applying that skill in her writing, you may want to switch her name with another student in order to use her piece as reinforcement. Explain this concept to your students. They will accept that you are in charge of making instructional decisions.

Show your students how their names will get turned over in their pocket on the sharing chart, to show that they have already shared this week. When all student's names have been turned over, the process begins again.

Follow Up

If your students continue to ask when they can share their writing, revisit this lesson. ■

Managing Journals

Materials: student journals

Prep Step: Some important decisions need to be made before presenting this lesson. Where will students keep their journals? How will they retrieve their journals when it is time to write? How will they put their journals away in an orderly fashion? What will they do when they have used all the pages of a journal? The following procedure describes decisions that we have made because they worked in our classrooms.

Procedure

In Sherra's classroom children are grouped in teams of four. Each team member's desk is color coded to match the colored bin where they store their journals. For example, the red team stores their journals in the red bin. When it is time to pass out the journals, a designated team captain is responsible for retrieving the bin and passing out the journals to his team members. That way a limited number of children are mobile. The storage bin stays with the team as they write. Journals are put away by reversing the process. All team members, with the exception of the people sharing, place their journals in the bin at the end of quiet-writing time. The team captain is responsible for putting the bin away as others move to the floor for sharing.

In Connie's room each child has a cloth pocket bag attached to their chair. When it is time to move from the mini-lesson to practice writing, the children simply retrieve their journals from their own pocket. She limits mobility by dismissing students selectively. For example, she may say that the children wearing red move first, then children with four letters in their name, next boys wearing tie shoes, etc. When quiet writing is over, all of her students return their journals to their chair backs with the exception of the sharing people.

Your students may keep their journals inside a desk rather than in a team bin. Or maybe each of your students has his own cubby and that's where you will choose to store the journals. The important thing about managing journals is that you explain the process to your students and then give them time to practice the actual movement.

> **GOAL**
>
> *To orderly manage the maintenance of writing journals*

Follow Up

Another issue you will want to address is what your students will do with their journals when there are no more blank pages. We like to make a simple flow chart or list of steps to assist the children with this process. Post this list where it will be convenient to revisit as needed. The list may look like this:

What To Do With Your Journal When It's Completely Filled In

1) Check your journal to be sure that you have used all the pages.

2) Place your journal in the blue tub next to the pencil sharpener for me to check. I will decide if that particular journal is going home or will be saved for a conference or portfolio.

3) Retrieve a new journal from the red tub on my desk. If for any reason our supply of new journals has run out, leave a note in the tub and write on a loose leaf piece of paper for that day.

Remember, when managing journals the process should fit the needs of your students, your teaching style, and the confines of your classroom. The important thing is to define your process clearly and then practice the steps that will allow the process to run smoothly. ■

Managing Writing Tools

Materials: writing tools (pencils, crayons, colored pencils, or pens), container with supply of spare sharpened pencils

Prep Step: None

Procedure

Discuss with your students which writing tools they can use during writer's workshop and why. For example, we allow our students to use colored pencils and gel pens, but we discuss how the pastel colors are hard to see: only bold, brilliant colors are acceptable. Markers are never used in their journals.

After this discussion, it is time to talk about what to do if your pencil breaks or your pen runs out of ink during practice-writing time. Ask your students what it would be like if someone used the pencil sharpener while the class was silently writing. You want them to understand that the noise of the pencil sharpener (or the noise of people moving around the room looking for another pen) would be distracting to others. It is also important to state that you want them to spend their writing time writing and nothing else.

> **GOAL**
>
> *To identify acceptable writing tools*

Show your students the container of spare sharpened pencils. Together, decide where in the room to keep it so it will be readily accessible to students. Explain that if their pencil breaks during writer's workshop (or if their pen stops working), they may silently help themselves to a pencil from the designated container. Have another container for where they return borrowed pencils. As the returns are sharpened, put them back in the container of spares.

Follow Up

Whenever the use of writing tools presents a problem, address alternatives during a mini-lesson. ∎

Silent/Quiet Writing

Materials: timer, chart paper, marker

Prep Step: None

Procedure

Engage your students in a discussion about how the words "silent" and "quiet" are different. Demonstrate the difference by having them sing the alphabet song quietly and then again silently in their heads.

Next, show them the timer and have them listen to its ring. Explain that after every mini-lesson we will have five minutes of silent writing followed by five minutes of quiet writing. (We have found that ten minutes total writing time is a good starting point for the beginning of kindergarten.) This time can and should be adjusted as the year progresses and your students mature.

You want to make clear that during silent writing there will be absolutely no talking. During quiet writing time only discussions pertaining to their writing will occur.

Follow Up

To help your students understand the concept of discussions that pertain to their writing, make a list of the types of talk you would expect to hear during quiet writing. Be sure to include non-examples. Also point out that there will be many times during quiet writing when talking will not be necessary. It is permissible only on a need-to-collaborate basis. A sample list is found below.

GOAL

To define the difference between silent and quiet writing, and to model what is appropriate to talk about during quiet writing

Examples of Quiet Writing Talk

1. "Please help me sound out the word beach."

2. "What letter do you hear at the end of school?"

3. "Read this sentence and tell me if it makes sense."

4. "Can you think of another word for 'went'?"

5. "Will you show me how to make a lower case k?"

6. "What would be a good title for this picture?"

Non-Examples of Quiet Writing Talk

1. "Are you going to Jim's birthday party?"

2. "I brought my lunch to school today."

3. "Do you know how to ride a bike with two wheels?"

4. "I have two dogs and one cat."

5. "I know how to spell my name."

6. "I can't find my crayon box." ∎

Practicing Transitions in Writer's Workshop

Materials: student journals, clipboards, writing tools, chart paper, marker

Prep Step: None

Procedure

In the course of writer's workshop, there are three transitions. Students are required to move to a gathering area for the mini-lesson, then to a writing area for practice, and finally back to the gathering area for sharing.

Identify a gathering area for your students. This will be a floor space large enough to allow all students to sit comfortably. Practice moving to the gathering area in different ways. For example, tiptoe to the gathering area, slink to the gathering area, walk very slowly, etc.

Decide in advance where you want your children to write during practice-writing time. Some teachers are more comfortable with everyone writing at their desk or table. Others allow students to write on the floor using clipboards. If you are uncertain, you may want to start with everyone at their desk or table and then move to limited choice.

Regardless of where they will be writing, students need to understand that it is their job to move to independent writing time both quietly and quickly. Only a short period of time is designated to the practice of writing and it may not be wasted looking for a place to write.

After the rules of "where to write" are defined, it is time to practice. Tell your students that you are going to time their movement from the floor to their writing spot. You will be looking for walking feet and listening for the sound of silence. You will stop timing them when everyone in the class has begun writing. Explain that every day, for the next five days, you will time their movement. Use the visual support of a graph to motivate students to improve their time each day. We have found that setting a class goal and then planning a way to celebrate if you reach that goal will motivate students to work as a team.

> ### GOAL
> *To transition efficiently from one activity to another*

The same process can be used to practice the final transition, when students move from their writing spot back to the gathering area. Some teachers have a designated signal or other clue to cue students. For example, turning off the lights or playing music can identify the transition time. It doesn't matter what cue you use as long as you are consistent.

Follow Up

Transition time lends itself to the introduction of similes, which make a comparison using the words "like" or "as." Brainstorm a list of things that are quiet and use them as a comparison for moving. For example, ask children to move to the gathering area "as quietly as falling snow." Whenever possible, use a simile to describe how the transition should be accomplished. ∎

Feedback

Materials: chart paper, markers

Prep Step: None

Procedure

Giving effective feedback is a skill best learned through modeling. Even though you may not formally introduce feedback until the third or fourth week of school, you will have been modeling how to give effective feedback since the beginning of the year. When the time comes to introduce feedback as a mini-lesson, you will want to start by defining what feedback is and why it is important to a writer.

Explain to your students that feedback is the information we give or the questions we ask after having heard a writer read a piece of their writing. Feedback should help the writer to improve her piece or her general writing technique.

Next, explain that feedback starts with "I noticed," "I liked," or a question word. It may also take the form of a reminder. On chart paper write the following examples:

When you wrote about loosing your tooth it reminded me of my loose tooth.

I noticed that you had a difficult time reading your sentence because you did not leave big enough spaces between the words.

I noticed that you labeled your pictures.

I liked your word choice. You used the word "fabulous" instead of a boring word like "fun."

I like the size of your words. They are not too big and not too small.

What does your dog look like?

How old were you on your birthday?

It would be best if the examples on the chart were authentic. Try using feedback given during yesterday's lesson.

GOAL

To model effective feedback

Spend a few minutes discussing how the feedback listed on the chart would help a writer to improve. For example, when Grace hears that the class noticed that she labeled her pictures, she will be encouraged to continue that practice.

Finally, tell your students that in the interest of time everyone won't be able to give feedback every day. We like to start the year by accepting one "I noticed" statement, one "I liked," and one question about each piece that is presented to the class. Depending on your class, this may or may not be increased as the year progresses.

Follow Up

The art of effective feedback will need to be continually modeled by the teacher and practiced by the students. ∎

Audience Etiquette

Materials: chart paper, markers

Prep Step: None

Note: This lesson should be done immediately after Operational Mini-Lesson 8.

Procedure

Remind your students that in order to offer effective feedback, they must first hear a writer's piece. This requires that they look like and sound like a good audience. Brainstorm the attributes of a good audience with your students, and record their answers on chart paper. Post the "Looks like/Sounds like" chart in the room and refer to it when necessary.

GOAL

To prepare a "Looks like/Sounds like" chart for audience etiquette

Follow Up

If students become lax in their audience etiquette, it will be necessary to return to the chart for review. ■

Sample Chart

A Good Audience Looks Like	A Good Audience Sounds Like
✓ children sitting on their bottoms	✓ children listening silently to the person who is sharing
✓ children sitting with their hands in their laps	✓ children offering feedback one at a time
✓ children with their eyes on the person who is sharing	✓ the teacher offering feedback
✓ children raising their hands to speak	

Conference Etiquette

Materials: None

Prep Step: None

Procedure

Engage your students in a conversation about conferencing by reminding them that at least once in the school year their parents will want to have a parent/teacher conference. "What do you think we will talk about during this conference? Who do you think will do the talking?"

Talk about how important it is for everyone to clearly communicate during this conference. What might happen if a student's parents don't understand what you, the teacher, is saying? What are some things that might make communication difficult during the conference?

Would it be acceptable for the teacher to be having a conference with Mary's mother and John's mother barges in and begins to have a conversation with the teacher? No, it wouldn't.

Explain that you will be talking with them several times a week about their writing. This is called a "writing conference." Help students understand that a writing conference may occur between the teacher and an individual student or the teacher and a small group. It may take place at a desk, at a table, or on the floor.

> **GOAL**
>
> *To define teacher expectations during writing conferences*

"We'll be following a process to make sure that I get to have a conference with everyone. However, it won't be possible to conference with everyone on the same day. So you'll have to wait patiently. When it's your turn, I'll come to you. And when it's your turn, the only thing we'll focus on is your writing. Interruptions aren't allowed."

During a group conference, you will invite them to join a small group to discuss a technique for improving their writing. Explain that you will always inform them ahead of time if they should be joining you for a group conference.

Follow Up

After practicing conferencing etiquette, reflect on the process with your whole class. Determine together what is working well and what needs to be changed. If problems occur, use a mini-lesson to address needed changes. ∎

Making Writing Mistakes

Materials: chart paper, markers, student samples when possible

Prep Step: None

Procedure

A teacher can learn a lot about a child by examining the child's mistakes. This is one good reason to purposefully teach children to cross through rather than erase their errors. Another reason not to erase is that it is a waste of valuable practice-writing time. Make children aware of both of these reasons by modeling these few examples on chart paper.

Examples:

I went to the beach with my mom and my sister ~~Elizab~~ Elizabeth.

(Explain how you crossed through, rather than erased, the word "Elizabeth" when you realized you did not have enough room to finish the word.)

I do ~~note~~ not want to go to the beach.

(Explain how you crossed through rather than erased the word "note" when you realized that the word you wanted to write was "not" with a short vowel sound and no silent "e" at the end.)

GOAL

To teach students to cross through—rather than erase—their errors

Begin to write a sentence and stop when you make a purposeful mistake. Tell your students that you want to erase the mistake. Ask them to watch the second hand on the clock to see how long it takes. Intentionally take a long time and erase hard enough to make a tear in the paper. Discuss the concept of wasted practice time with your students.

Finally, tell your class that you will be looking for students who remember to cross through rather than erase mistakes. As authentic examples arise, be sure to compliment the individual and share their example with the whole class.

Follow Up

Whenever you write in front of the class, take opportunities to model crossing through mistakes. ∎

How to Share Your Writing

Materials: chart paper, marker

Prep Step: Prepare a piece of your own writing to share

Procedure

Decide ahead of time where you want your children to stand or sit when they share their writing. Some teachers like to have a special sharing chair or podium for the students to use. Others simply ask students to stand in front of the audience. Whatever your preference, it is important to model both examples and non-examples of what good sharing looks like and sounds like.

GOAL

To model appropriate sharing practices

Start by sharing your own piece. Tell students that you would like them to raise their hands if they see or hear any problems. Begin to read with the paper held in front of your face, blocking your mouth and eyes. As students notice the

problem, stop for discussion. Then model the correct position for the paper to be held.

Move on to model other inappropriate sharing practices. For example, you could speak too softly, read too quickly, read too slowly, or wiggle around while you are reading. Each time a problem is identified, stop for discussion and model the way it should look and sound.

Follow Up

To help students understand good sharing practices, make a "Looks like/Sounds like" chart similar to the sample chart made in Operational Mini-Lesson 9. Hang the chart in your classroom and refer to it whenever necessary. ■

Buddy Conferences

Materials: a writing piece from each child, chart paper, markers

Prep Step: None

Procedure

There will be times throughout the year when you will want children to be able to share their writing with one classmate rather than the whole group. We call this "buddy sharing."

Explain to your students that sometimes it will be better to get feedback from just one classmate rather than from the entire class. Define a process for selecting a partner and moving to a sharing space. Partner selection can be accomplished in a variety of ways and does not have to be done the same way every time. For example, students may be paired at random, by like abilities, or heterogeneously. Move to a place in the room that is conducive to sharing.

The first time you have your students practice buddy sharing, show them how to sit face to face on the floor. Talk about the importance of looking at your partner as they share their piece. When someone is looking at you, it is a clue that they are listening to what you are saying.

> ### GOAL
> *To define and use a process for sharing writing with one person*

Also discuss the importance of taking turns: one person is speaking while the other person is listening. This is a good time to review audience etiquette and effective feedback.

As you finish your first practice, come together as a group to have a quick discussion about how buddy sharing went.

Follow Up

Create a plus/delta chart with your students about the buddy sharing process. Begin with the positive statements: "What went well?" Record these under the plus side of your two-column chart. Move to the negative statements: "What needs to be improved?" Record these under the delta side. Use this information to make any necessary changes to your class's buddy-sharing process. ∎

Adding On to a Previous Piece

Materials: a sample writing piece on chart paper that the teacher started but did not finish the day before

Prep Step: None

Procedure

Assure your students that you are aware that they do not always have time to finish a piece of writing in one writer's workshop. Show the class the story you started yesterday, but did not finish. Review what you have done so far:

✓ drew a picture of the playground

✓ labeled the slide, swings, and merry-go-round

✓ wrote a sentence

Explain to your students that you knew you wanted to tell more about your sentence, but you ran out of time. Now you can't remember what it is you wanted to write. How can you help yourself remember what you were thinking? Reread!

Reread the sentence from yesterday. "I like to slide down the slide." Then tell your students that rereading has helped you remember that you wanted to write about going down the slide backwards and bumping your head! Add this elaboration to yesterday's sentence.

Remind your students that you would not have remembered what you wanted to write had you not reread your work. Challenge them to begin their journal writing today by rereading their own work from a previous day. Choose one person to demonstrate the rereading process for the whole class.

> ### GOAL
> *To add on to a previous writing piece*

Follow Up

Continue to challenge students to begin journal writing by rereading their own work. ■

Introducing a Rubric

Materials: chart paper, marker, blank paper for each child, crayons, blue, red, and green stickers

Prep Step: None

Procedure

Ask your students to draw a flower on a sheet of paper. Give no instructions except "draw a flower." Share with the students that you will be moving around the room, awarding blue stickers to some flowers and red and green stickers to the other flowers. Give no further instructions about how you will decide which students will be awarded which stickers.

As the students draw, place the various color stickers on their papers. Place blue stickers only on the drawings that have 1) a flower of multiple colors 2) a stem and leaf and 3) background. Do not share these expectations with the class. Make only general comments like, "I like your flower" or "Those sure are pretty colors." Give no specific feedback.

When all students are finished call them to the gathering area. Ask the children who received blue stickers to stand. Explain that the children with blue stickers drew the kind of flower that you were looking for. Now ask the children with red and green stickers to stand. Tell them that you think their flowers are nice, but just not the kind you wanted.

Point out that you did not share your expectations for receiving a blue sticker before they started drawing. Ask if it would have been easier to receive a blue sticker if you had. Discuss the importance of having expectations clearly defined before attempting any task.

Divide a large sheet of chart paper into thirds.

GOAL

To demonstrate the importance of knowing expectations before attempting a task

Put a blue sticker in the first section, and explain that you are going to draw a blue-sticker flower so everyone will know what a blue-sticker flower is. Draw a large flower with six petals, a stem, and a leaf. Color the petals different colors and add some grass and a sun. Ask the class what they notice about your drawing. Record their observations under the picture. Again have the children who received blue stickers stand and re-examine their drawings to determine if they did indeed meet the criteria.

In the second section, place a red sticker. Draw a flower with four petals, a stem, and no leaf. Color the petals with two colors and add grass and a sun. Ask the red-sticker children to stand. Determine what they would need to do to make their flower a blue-sticker flower.

In the third section, place a green sticker. Draw a flower with no petals and a stem. Color the flower all one color. Do not include anything in the background. Ask the green-sticker children to stand. Determine what they would need to do to make their flower a blue-sticker flower.

Repeat that it would have been much easier for everyone to draw a blue-sticker flower if you had shared your expectations ahead of time. Explain that these written expectations are called "rubrics."

"Rubrics help us because they define what is expected of us. Sometimes rubrics even have pictures called 'anchor pictures' to go with them. They help learners to know what the expectations are for quality work. Tomorrow, everyone will have the opportunity to draw a blue-sticker flower. Won't it be easier now that you know what a blue-sticker flower is?"

Follow Up

Collect the flower pictures so you can hand them out again the next day. Using the rubric you defined during the previous day's writer's workshop, have your students use the back of the paper to draw a blue-sticker flower. ■

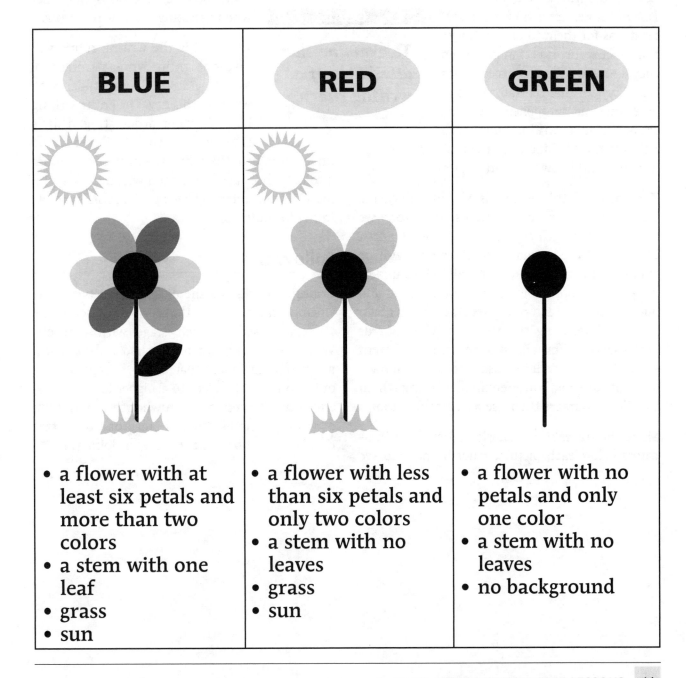

BLUE	RED	GREEN
• a flower with at least six petals and more than two colors • a stem with one leaf • grass • sun	• a flower with less than six petals and only two colors • a stem with no leaves • grass • sun	• a flower with no petals and only one color • a stem with no leaves • no background

Examining the Attributes of a Rubric

Materials: your district's writing rubric or sample rubric included with this lesson

Prep Step: None

Procedure

Remind your students of the flower rubric you developed during Operational Mini-Lesson 15. Reinforce how much easier it was for them to draw a flower that met your expectations when they knew what your expectations were. Explain that the same sorts of guidelines can be applied to writing skills. Using a writing rubric will help them determine how accomplished they are as writers, and how they can improve.

The focus of this lesson is sharing a writing rubric. Use either your district's or the one we have included with this lesson. We developed it by rewriting the language of our district's writing rubric so it was easier for our children to understand. We wrote the guidelines out by hand and added pictures. Each of the six stages has its own page, and we hang them on our white boards with magnets. This allows us to remove different stages from the wall for discussion or to show a student during conferencing. Making them mobile encourages their use as a teaching tool.

Share the stages of the rubric and read the indicators below each picture. Students need to see anchor papers in the form of a rubric. Spending time articulating the strengths and weaknesses of an anchor paper will assist students in identifying how and if expectations were met when assessing their own writing.

GOAL

To examine the attributes of a writing rubric

Introducing the writing rubric will take one entire writer's workshop. We do not send our students to write on this day. The entire writing block is spent articulating. This is time well spent. Children must understand how the rubric works so they can use it to help them apply it to their writing. We spend many lessons referring back to the rubric after its initial introduction.

Follow Up

Continue to discuss the differences between the writing stages. Invite the class to discuss the strategies used in each stage with partners. Whenever writing pieces are shared and discussed, point out attributes that could be changed in order to move the piece to a higher level. In general, students need to learn what the continuum of writing feels like from a stage one to a stage five. Use the rubric as a vehicle for doing this. ■

Stage 1A

MkMeЯHeIHaKNapS2szrętyKpOyyjy

- Drawing or Scribbling
- Random letters or strings

Stage 1B

I ꓱ O M B

- Uses beginning sounds.
- Labels drawings

Stage 2

I fl of my bik win I was
going to fast it hrt bad

- Writes at least one big thought
- Anyone can read it without your help
- Words go from left to right
- Uses temporary spelling
- Uses spaces between words
- Uses some correctly spelled sight words

Stage 3

I fel off my bik wen I was going
to fast. It hrt bad. it was a
tawny in bik It is pyk It is Big

- Writes at least two big thoughts
  that go together
- Uses specific details
- Uses some periods and capital letters

Stage 4

On Sunday when I was riding my
pink bike to fast I fell off.
I landid on the side walk.
I brusde my ne My mom said
are you all right. I said I am
bleeding my mom put a bandad
on Me then I got back on my
bike and I ridedid my bike home.

- Writes at least three big ideas that go together
- Tells more about the previous sentence by
  elaborating on at least one big idea
- Uses a simple beginning, middle, and end

Stage 5

I fell befor and so have you. Wen I fell I was riding my pink bike at my grandmas and my cusins were thar My cusins names were Susen, billy, and Jakup. We wrer racing our bikes outside and I had fancy shoes on. they wrer slepry. I was pedling and my sho slept. and I was smiling and I had a loose tooth and I fell on it and I felt like it was going up and down. I was bleeting and I stod up and started to Scream and I ran to my mom. She helpt me rins out my mouth and sav my tooth in a small white envalop. I put the tooth under my pillo. I woneder if the tooth fare will come?

- Tells more about the sentence before elaborating on more than one big idea
- Uses writer's tricks to make their piece sound better
- All sentences don't start the same way

Assessing Writing Using a Rubric

Materials: writing rubric, student samples, sticky notes

Prep Step: None

Procedure

Place all the stages of the writing rubric in the center of the floor. Make sure they are visible to all students. Review the indicators for each stage.

Share a piece of student writing by reading it aloud. As the children become more proficient at scoring papers, reading it aloud will be sufficient, but for this first mini-lesson also write it on a sheet of chart paper or put it on the overhead.

Ask students to determine what stage of writing the piece is most like. Have them hold up a finger to indicate its stage. Invite a few students to share their thinking about why they chose the stage they did. Reach a consensus with the group. Place the piece underneath the correct stage.

Repeat the procedure with several different samples at different stages. This is another mini-lesson in which we don't send our students for individual writing practice. This discussion should encompass an entire writing block.

GOAL

To assess a piece of writing using a writing rubric

Follow Up

To reinforce using the rubric as an assessment tool, invite several students to bring their own writing to the gathering area. Together help the author determine which stage his piece represents. Make a revision plan that would raise the piece to the next level. Record this plan on a sticky note. Keep it simple. An example might be to write a letter for every sound. Place the sticky note in the author's journal for him as a reference for revision.

Use several sessions to practice with the rubric. Continue to use the rubric as an instructional tool during conferencing and sharing. Remind students to use the rubric as a reference when they are writing. Invite students of other grades to share their writing with the group and assign a writing stage to the piece together. Remember to share the rubric with parents during Open House or conferences. ∎

Making a Plan for Improving Writing

Materials: classroom rubric, individual rubrics, pencil

Prep Step: None

Procedure

Day One

Instruct students to choose one of their best writing pieces from their journals. Tell them to mark that page and bring it to the gathering place. Place the classroom rubric on the floor where it is visible to all students.

GOAL

To make a writing improvement plan

As each student shares their piece of writing, decide as a class which stage of the writing rubric it most resembles. (Having the entire class share at once is only possible near the beginning of kindergarten. Later, you will need to spend more than one mini-lesson sharing pieces.)

After everyone has had a chance to share, give each child a copy of the individual rubric included with this lesson. (Note the individual rubric only goes through stage four in interest of space. If you want your students to see stage five, it would need to be printed on a separate page.) Have each child mark an X on the box that matches their stage.

Day Two

Gather your students around the rubric again. Read through the indicators underneath each stage. Discuss the strategies writers would need to move their writing to the next stage. Writing a piece at the next stage should be their goal.

Next, have each student share one of the strategies they will focus on during the next three months. This becomes a plan for improving their writing. The plan will be recorded on the individual rubric during conferencing. There may be several children who need to work on writing sentences. Have those students stand up together. Other children may need to work on using periods or capital letters, have those children stand together and so on. Make sure students know which strategy is best for them to concentrate on.

Follow Up

Instruct students to have their individual rubrics ready during quiet writing. As you conference with them, record their plan. You will need to determine how often you want to repeat this mini-lesson to develop new action plans. We develop new plans in January and May. Share these plans with parents during conferences. ■

Writing

Name_____

End of year expectations are for student to be writing at stage _____.

January goal_____   May goal_____

Action Plan_____   Action Plan_____

_____   _____

	Sept.	Jan.	May
Stage 4 Three big ideas, elaboration, beginning, middle, end, glitter words			
Stage 3 Two big thoughts, details, periods, capital letters			
Stage 2 One big thought, can be read, left to right, temporary spelling, spaces, sight words			
Stage 1B Use beginning sounds, labels			
Stage 1A Drawing, scribbling, mock letters			

On Sunday when I was riding my pink bike to fast I fell off. I landid on the side walk. I brusde my ne My mom said are you all right. I said I am bleeding my mom put a bandad on Me then I got back on my bike and I ridedid my bike home.

I fel off my bik wen I was going to fast. It hrt bad. it was a tawny in bik It is pyk It is Big

I fl of my bik win I was going to fast it hrt bad

I ꓊ O M B

Print Awareness Mini-Lessons

Target Skills Addressed

- managing space

- spaces between words

- left-to-right

- top-to-bottom

- return sweep

- letter-sound correspondence

- word families

- temporary spelling

- periods

- question marks

- quotation marks

- capital letters

Temporary or Invented Spelling

Materials: chart paper, markers

Prep Step: None

Procedure

Discuss with your students how people are not perfect the first time they attempt any task. Remind them that it takes many attempts to learn how to tie shoes or jump rope. Perfect is not important, practice is! The only way to get better at anything is to keep practicing.

Explain to your students that at their age they do not know how to spell many words correctly. Throughout the year you will be working on spelling patterns and sight words, so you should assure them that their spelling will improve with time. In the meanwhile, it is important for them to continue to work on their writing skills. They will not learn to write simple stories or even sentences if they are afraid to attempt words that they do not know how to spell correctly. Explain that spelling a word by simply writing the letter sounds they hear in that word is not only acceptable, it's expected.

Next, play a game we call "How Do You Spell?" Tell your students that you are going to call out a very big word that you are sure they will not know how to spell. A good word to start with is "butterfly." Segment the word slowly, asking students to say every sound they hear. After each letter they give, repeat the word. For example, when a student identifies that there is a "B" at the beginning, write the letter "B" and then repeat the word asking for the sound that comes next. Accept all answers without correction.

Continue this game using several more "big" words. You may want to call volunteers to the chart paper to be the writer. Keep the mood light and humorous. For example, after each spelling we do a little chant about that word: "I'm not afraid to spell 'butterfly.' 'Butterfly' doesn't scare me!"

GOAL

To encourage students to use temporary spelling in their writing

Remember, the idea is to promote temporary spelling which will allow children to take risks in their writing. Children who are hesitant to use temporary spelling will produce threadbare writing because they will be confined to the few words they are able to spell correctly. When you give children the freedom to spell incorrectly, you allow them the room to grow as emergent writers.

Follow Up

Keep playing variations of "How Do You Spell?" until your class is comfortable using temporary spelling in their writing. For example, you may call out "big" words as your students write the sounds they hear on white boards or paper. This method allows them to compare their attempts with a neighbor.

You may even want to give a temporary spelling test. Young students get excited about the idea of taking a test. Call out the words, collect the papers, and reward everyone with a sticker or happy face. Spend a minute discussing why they all received happy faces even though they may have spelled the words a little differently. The expectation is that everyone tried to spell by recording a letter for every sound they heard. ∎

Every Sound Needs a Letter

Materials: chart paper, markers

Prep Step: None

Procedure

At the top left of a sheet of chart paper, write the letter "L." Tell your students that "L" is the first letter of the word that you are thinking about. Ask students to guess what word you have in mind. List five guesses on chart paper. Is there any way to be sure which word you had in mind if the only clue is the first letter? Of course not! Now give the second letter. Through the process of comparing the words, see when they can guess the word you were thinking about. It works best if a few of the words on the list have at least the first two letters in common. For example:

> ### GOAL
> *To demonstrate the importance of writing a letter for every sound*

1. love
2. lollipop
3. like
4. little
5. lunch

As they compare the words your students will discover that they need a third letter, or maybe even the last letter, in order to guess your word.

Now make the connection between this activity and temporary spelling. Remind students that temporary spelling is simply writing down the sounds they hear in a word. However, if they only write down the first letter in a word, it will be impossible for anyone else to read their work. Use the following example to ground your point. Write the letter "b" on the chart paper. Ask students if they are able to read your word. Then write the letters "b-i-k" on the chart paper. Now is there anyone who can read my word? Explain that "bik" is not the correct way to spell "bike," but there are enough letters and sounds that go together to make it readable.

Conclude with this reminder: When you are trying to spell a word, repeat that word, out loud if necessary, as many times as it takes to hear all of the sounds.

Follow Up

Repeat the process in this lesson using different letters and words. ■

Letters Make Words/Words Make Sentences

Materials: chart paper, markers, a sentence strip, glue stick

Prep Step: None

Procedure

At the top of a sheet of chart paper scatter the following letters:

Explain to your students that you want them to help you use these letters to make words. The first word you want to write is "my." Elicit their help in sounding out the word "my." In this case you want to help them use correct spelling. You are engaged in a guided writing with the whole class.

Write the word "my" on the chart paper under the scattered letters. Cross out the letters "m" and "y." Follow the same procedure to spell "is," "brown," and "cat" in that order. Write the words in list form, and cross out the scattered letters as you go. Remind your students that you are putting letters together to make words.

Now read the list. Ask your students if there is any way we can string these four words together

> ### GOAL
>
> *To practice using letters to make words and words to make sentences*

to create a sentence that makes sense. When they conclude that the words make a sentence if you say them in a certain order—"My cat is brown"—write that sentence on a sentence strip.

Read the sentence to your students again, and remind them that you put letters together to make the words, and words together to make the sentence. Then cut apart the words on the sentence strip. Pass the words to four students. Ask the person holding the word "my" to come up to the chart paper. Tell them that you want to put the sentence back together. "Where should we glue the word 'my'?" Help them to glue the first word of the sentence all the way to the left. Continue calling for the other words, helping students to leave appropriate spaces between the words as they glue. Use a marker to add a period at the end of the sentence. Read the sentence with your class.

Follow Up

Repeat the process in this lesson using different letters to spell different words and sentences. ■

Spaces Between Words

Materials: chart paper, markers

Prep Step: Prepare a poster or chart by writing the text of any simple, familiar nursery rhyme.

Procedure

Show your students a printed nursery rhyme on a chart or poster. Read it to them once and then invite them to read it with you. Tell them that you want to write this nursery rhyme on your own piece of paper. At the top left of a sheet of chart paper begin to write the nursery rhyme. Leave no spaces between words, and use no other writing conventions. For example, if you were using "Jack and Jill," you would write

jackandjillwentupthehilltofetchapailofwater

jackfelldownandbrokehiscrown

andjillcametumblingafter

Ask a student to read the rhyme as you've written it. Point out how difficult it is for the reader to know where one word ends and the next begins when there are no spaces between the words. Rewrite the entire rhyme. Encourage the children to tell you where to leave spaces, and model using capital letters and periods where appropriate.

Briefly discuss how conventions help the reader make sense of the text. However, remember that the focus of your lesson is leaving spaces between words.

> **GOAL**
>
> *To model how to leave spaces between words*

Follow Up

You will want to share strategies with your students to help them remember to leave spaces. Showing them how to put down a spacer—their fingers, a Popsicle stick, or a craft stick—whenever they finish writing a word will help them know where to start writing the next word. We call spacer-sticks "spacemen," and we allow students to decorate them with marker and use them whenever they write. ▪

Managing Space on a Page

Materials: chart paper, markers

Prep Step: None

Procedure

The best way to model how to manage space—including left-to-right orientation, return sweep, and top-to-bottom—is to show your students how it is not done. Start by writing a few sentences on chart paper that do not demonstrate the correct management of space.

GOAL

To model how to manage space on a page

is

My name

Mrs.

Jones.

I teach kindergarten

Point to the words as you read the sentences out loud. See if you can elicit from your students what is wrong with your writing. Compliment their ideas as you move forward with your demonstration.

Rewrite the sentences, pointing out that you start at the top left, move to the right, and then return all the way to the left when you run out of room. Call their attention to the fact that we write in the same direction as we read. Continue elaborating your story until you come to the bottom of the page. Explain that only when you come to the bottom do you move to another sheet of paper.

Now start a second piece. Before you begin writing, pose the following questions to your students:

✓ Where should I begin my writing?

  ✓ Where will I move after that?

  ✓ What will I do when I come to the end of the first line?

  ✓ When will I move to a new sheet of paper?

  ✓ Does it matter how big my letters are?

Try to make the lesson almost silly. Play with your students. Pretend that you are going to start writing at the bottom of the page or in the middle of the paper. Write your letters super big or ridiculously small. Allow them to correct your silly errors.

Conclude by reminding students that following certain rules is what makes it possible to read other's texts.

Follow Up

During conferencing, make note of students not managing space on a page. It may be helpful to provide those students with the structured lined paper found with Print Awareness Mini-Lesson 12, which provides visual guidelines to assist in managing space. ■

The First Word of a Sentence Has a Capital Letter

Materials: alphabet strip with capital and lower-case letters, chart paper, markers

Prep Step: None

Procedure

Start by showing students the alphabet strip. Discuss how every letter of the alphabet is written two ways, "upper case" (or "capital") and "lower case." Explain that the first word of every sentence starts with a capital letter. Tell your students that you are going to write several sentences together to demonstrate this concept.

> **GOAL**
>
> *To capitalize the first letter of a sentence*

Start your story with this sentence: "Yesterday, I brought my lunch to school." Use a red marker to write the letter "Y" in "yesterday" and a blue marker for the rest of the letters. Write the word "I" in red since it is always capitalized. Make mention of that fact, but remember that the focus of this lesson is starting sentences with capital letters. Move to the next sentence following the same procedure. When you are finished, your chart paper will look something like this:

Yesterday, I brought my lunch to school. My mom packed my favorite sandwich, peanut butter and jelly. My best friend Kelly had peanut butter and jelly too. We laughed about how the peanut butter sticks to your mouth. Thank goodness we had cold milk to wash it down.

Again, color code the word "I" and the proper noun "Kelly." Simply mention to students why you are capitalizing those words, but do not lose the focus of your lesson.

Count the sentences. Point out to students that you know where one sentence stops and another starts because of the periods. After every period, you should find a word that starts with a capital letter.

Follow Up

Reinforce this lesson by asking students to highlight the words starting with capital letters in any copied text. Review the words together. ∎

Where Do You Put a Period?

Materials: four sentence strips, four small index cards, chart paper, markers

Prep Step: None

Procedure

Interview one child about his pet. Ask the following four questions: "What kind of pet do you have? What is its name? What color is your pet? Where does your pet usually sleep?"

Help the student answer each question in a complete sentence. As the student answers each question, write the sentences down on four separate sentence strips, but leave off the periods. Remind students that words go together to make a complete thought that we call a "sentence." Hand the sentence strips to any four students and ask them to line up in the order that the sentences were written. They should hold the strips so the rest of the class can read them.

Count the sentences. After you count four sentences, explain that four periods are needed, one for the end of each sentence. "A period is the signal that tells the reader to stop. It is how the reader knows that one sentence is finished and another is about to begin." Before inserting the periods, read the sentences without stopping in between.

> **GOAL**
>
> *To identify the period as the signal for ending a statement*

Make four large periods on four separate index cards. Pass out the cards to four more students. See if they can place themselves into the line in the appropriate places. Once there is a period at the end of each sentence, reread the sentences, stopping when you see the periods.

Ask the students holding the periods to sit down in the line. Invite the audience to read the sentences with you without stopping in between. Then have the students who are holding the periods stand back up. As a class, reread the sentences, stopping at the periods.

Follow Up

Reinforce this lesson by asking students to highlight the periods found in any copied text. After highlighting, have them count the sentences. ■

When Do You Use a Question Mark Instead of a Period?

Materials: chart paper, two color markers, paper or sentence strip, pencils

Prep Step: None

Procedure

Through discussion, help your students understand that a question is a request for information. Point out that when someone asks a question, an answer is expected. Give several examples. Then list the following five words on chart paper, leaving enough space to write a question after each word:

Who _____

What _____

Where _____

When _____

Why _____

Ask children to help you think of questions that start with each of these words. At the end of each sentence use a different color marker to write the question mark. "A question mark, like a period, tells the reader to stop. But it also tells the reader that a request for information has been made."

GOAL

To identify a question mark as the signal for ending a question

Follow Up

Ask your students to participate in a quick-write. Give each a sheet of paper or a sentence strip and ask them to write one question directed to anyone in the classroom. Remind them to start their question with a capital letter and end it with a question mark. During group share, have each writer read their question, and have the appropriate person answer. If possible, hang the questions around the room to serve as reminders. ∎

Every Word Has a Vowel

Materials: alphabet strip, chart paper, markers, highlighter

Prep Step: None

Procedure

Review the alphabet strip with your students. Point out the vowels and the consonants. Count the vowels, and then count the consonants. Explain to students that in English, every word has at least one vowel. Challenge them to give you a word that does not have a vowel by allowing students to call out words as you write them on chart paper. Choose a volunteer to highlight the vowels in each word. Point out that vowels can come at the beginning, middle, or end of a word.

> **GOAL**
>
> *To identify vowels and consonants in words*

Follow Up

Discuss how sometimes a vowel can say its own name. When that happens, it is called a long vowel sound. "Acorn," "eagle," "play," "tree," and "icicle," all have long vowel sounds. But sometimes words have what we call a short vowel sound. "Apple," "hot," "wind," "tent," and "under" all have short vowel sounds. List examples on chart paper.

Conclude by reminding students to be sure they try to include vowels in every word they write. ■

Words With Long Vowels	Words With Short Vowels
acorn	apple
people	pepper
pie	little
oval	octopus
unicorn	puppy

Words Have Families, Too!

Materials: chart paper, markers, magnetic letters ("b," "c," "f," "h," "m," "p," "r," "s," "a," and "t"), magnetic board

Prep Step: None

Procedure

On a sheet of chart paper list the first and last names of members of your own immediate family. Ask your students what is the same about all of these names. Discuss how people in the same family often have last names in common. Demonstrate how words have families by making a list of words in the "At" family.

bat	mat
cat	pat
fat	rat
hat	sat

Read the words and then discuss how they are alike and how they are different. Why are they considered to be in the same family? Be sure to point out that these words share a spelling pattern. "Once you know the pattern, you only need to change the beginning to make a new word."

Place the magnetic "a" and "t" in the center of your magnetic board. Scatter the consonants "b," "c," "f," "h," "m," "p," "r," and "s" randomly around the edges of the board. Ask for volunteers to help you make words. For example, call on someone to select the letter that will make the word "sat." Continue until all possibilities are exhausted.

GOAL

To introduce spelling patterns

Follow Up

Assemble one plastic bag per child filled with the following: a square piece of paper with "__ a t" written on the front and one small square of paper for each of the letters "b," "c," "f," "h," "m," "p," "r," and "s" (one letter per square).

Pass out the bags. Call out "at" words and ask your students to manipulate the letter squares to build the word you are calling. Later, when students move to their journals, ask them to participate in a quick-write by listing as many "at" words as they can in three minutes.

Duplicate this activity using any spelling pattern. ■

Our Names Start with Capital Letters

Materials: chart paper, markers, clipboards, a highlighter for each student

Prep Step: Prepare a chart that lists the first names of all the students in your class. Also prepare a copy of the included Bingo sheet and nine bingo chips for each student.

Procedure

Display the chart paper that lists every child's first name. Highlight the first letter of each name as you point out that all of our names begin with a capital letter, and that the rest of the letters are usually lower case.

Every primary classroom has student names displayed in a variety of ways and places. Ask a few volunteers to help you look around the room for places where names are written. Help your students identify these places as sources where they could go to copy the names of their classmates.

Show students the Bingo game sheet. Explain to them that they are to write one of their classmate's names in each of the empty boxes. They may use clipboards and pencils as they walk around the room copying names. Each game sheet will have a total of nine names. Remind them to pay special attention to using capital and lower case letters correctly.

GOAL

To recognize that every name begins with a capital letter

When they've chosen nine of their classmate's names and filled them in on their game sheets, the students should return to their seats and highlight the capital letter at the beginning of each name on their sheet. Then they are ready to play the game.

Give nine bingo chips to each student. (We put them in plastic bags and pass those out to the students.) Randomly call out the names of the students in your class (or hold up printed name cards for everyone to see). If a student has written the name you called on their game sheet, then they get to place a chip on that square. The first person to fill up their game sheet yells "BINGO!" ■

Your Name	Name Bingo	Date
	Directions: Fill each blank box with the name of one of your classmates. Be sure that the first letter of their name is capitalized and all of the other letters are lower case. Highlight all of the capital letters on your paper. Now we are ready to play Name Bingo!	

Left-to-Right/Top-to-Bottom

Materials: pencils

Prep Step: As with most of the mini-lessons in this book, this can be directed at your whole class or targeted to a small group of students. Make a copy of the structured lined paper included with this lesson for everyone that is participating.

Procedure

Many young children have a difficult time understanding where to begin writing on the paper and/or internalizing left-to-right orientation. Use the structured lined paper to model this awareness of print concept.

Begin by pointing out the bold line on the left margin of the paper. Help children identify the left margin by teaching them to trace over that line with their finger before they begin to write. This is the line that will guide every return sweep.

Begin to write. Show them how you start at the top left, by the star on the structured lined paper.

GOAL

To model where to begin writing on the page and left-to-right orientation

Demonstrate what you do when you come to the end of a line. Model how to fill the entire page. "Remember, you will not start on another sheet of paper until you reach the bottom of this sheet."

Offer this structured paper to any child who is having difficulty with these concepts.

Follow Up

Continue to offer this paper to any child who is having difficulty with these concepts. ∎

*

Guided Drawing/Segmentation

Materials: a piece of chart paper with eight boxes with lines drawn like the guided drawing paper included with this lesson, marker, pencils

Prep Step: Copy the guided drawing paper for each student.

Procedure

Have your students bring pencils and clipboards to the gathering area. Pass out the guided drawing paper found on page 89. Explain that they will be drawing pictures in the boxes on the left and then writing the words that name each picture in the boxes on the right.

Model how to draw a picture in the top left-hand box. The picture should be something easy such as a line, a house, a dot, a kite, etc.

After drawing the picture, have the group say the word that represents it. Practice segmenting the word by counting how many sounds the group hears in it. In the box at the right, model how to make a line for each sound in the word. For example, a picture of a kite in the top left box would require three lines in the top right box because there are three sounds in that word.

Model how to fill in each line with the letter that represents the sound. The important skill your students are practicing is listening for sounds, so temporary spelling is expected. Model the exercise on your easel, reminding your students to "say it again," after each written letter.

Continue until all of the boxes are full.

Follow Up

GOAL

To practice segmenting words into sounds

You can vary this lesson by providing segmentation sheets for each student. Example reproducibles are found on pages 90 to 92. Although these three sheets will probably not provide enough practice for mastery, you can produce your own practice books using simple pictures such as these.

Provide each child with their own three-prong folder that contains segmentation sheets. Unlike the guided drawing paper, these sheets already have simple pictures drawn on the left side. On the right side, the lines are pre-drawn to scaffold segmentation of the sounds. Practice can be done as a whole group, a small group, or individually. ■

_ _ _ _ _ _ _

_ _ _ _ _ _ _ _

_ _ _ _ _ _ _ _

_ _ _ _ _ _

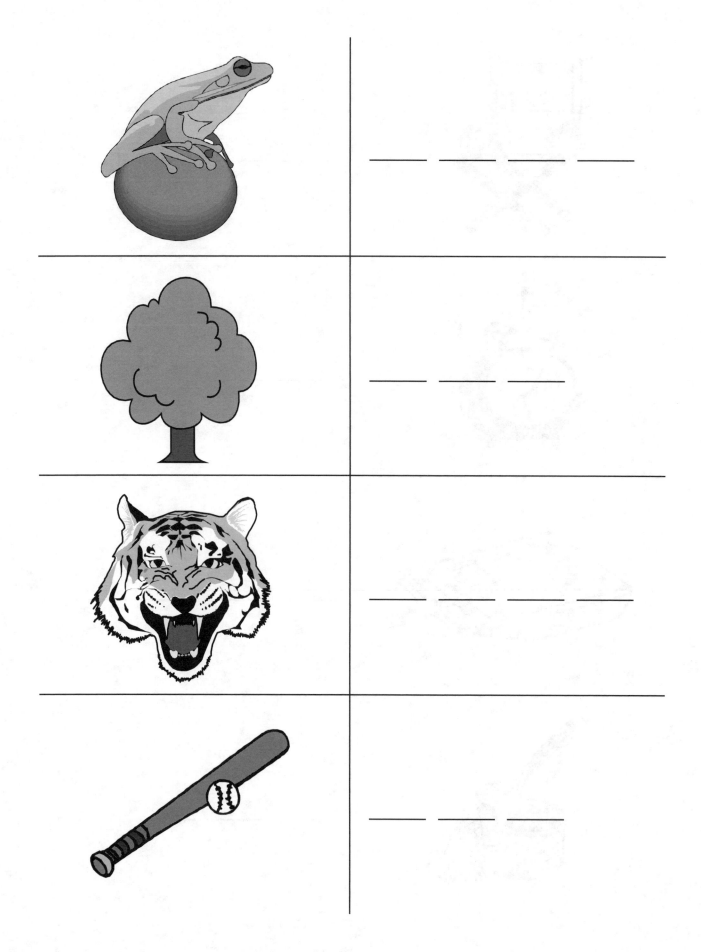

Using Quotation Marks

Materials: index cards, three sentence strips, scissors, marker

Prep Step: Prepare two index cards, one with the left-hand side of a pair of quotation marks, one with the right-hand side. Also prepare three index cards with the following prewritten questions:

1. How old are you?   2. What grade are you in?   3. What is your last name?

Procedure

Place the three index cards with prewritten questions in a bag, box, or tub. Ask for a volunteer to pick a question-card out of the bag. Read the question and help the student answer it in a complete sentence. Write exactly what the child said on a sentence strip, purposefully leaving off the quotation marks, but including a speaker attribution. For example:

I am five years old said Jim.

Show the class the two index cards with the quotation marks. Explain that you would like to use these marks to capture or catch only the part of the sentence that Jim said—the words that actually came out of his mouth. "These marks are called 'speaker tags.' They tag the words that the speaker said. You could cut the rest of the words off, and you wouldn't lose anything that Jim actually said."

Guide your students into telling you to cut off the words "said Jim." Set those words to the side and ask Jim to stand in front of the class holding the words that actually came out of his mouth. Then allow two volunteers to "capture" Jim's words by standing with the quotation marks at the beginning and end of "I am five years old."

GOAL

To identify quotation marks as speaker tags

Have a final volunteer stand with the cut-off attribution at the end of the line.

So there should be four students in front of the class:

Student 1, holding an index card with a quotation mark

Student 2 (Jim), holding his words

Student 3, holding an index card with a quotation mark

Student 4, holding the end of the sentence ("said Jim")

Repeat the above process two more times using sentences that answer the other two questions.

Follow Up

Use any Big Book for shared reading that demonstrates the use of quotation marks in real text. We use *Mrs. Wishy Washy* by Joy Cowley. ∎

Foundational Mini-Lessons

Target Skills Addressed

- choosing a topic
- beginning, middle and end
- leads
- endings
- focus
- transition words
- setting
- character development
- sequencing
- titles

Writing as Communication

Materials: chart paper, marker, paper, crayons, pencils

Prep Step: None

Procedure

Call the children to the gathering area in front of an easel. Explain that there will be a time every day when they will practice their writing. Tell them that this time even has a special name. This writing time is called "writer's workshop."

A workshop is a place where something is being built. During writer's workshop they will be building their writing skills. Specify that writing is a way to let other people know what you are thinking, so it's a very important way to communicate.

Explain that they will be learning more about what writer's workshop looks like and sounds like on another day. But for today, what they really need to understand is that writer's workshop is the time and place they will work on their writing.

Draw a quick picture of yourself on the easel. Do not tell the class who you are drawing. Ask for volunteers to share who they think the drawing might be. Accept all responses. Then share that the person on the chart is you! Ask how you could make sure everyone knows that picture is you.

> **GOAL**
>
> *To define writing as a form of communication*

"I could write my name under the picture, couldn't I?" Do that, saying each letter as you write. Explain that by writing your name under the picture you are confident that everyone would know that it is you. Also explain that the words are carrying a message: This picture is a picture of you!

Give each student a blank sheet of paper and ask them to draw a picture of themselves. Tell them to write their names beneath their pictures.

Share each student's self-portrait and read their name. Students who cannot write their names should write the letters they know. Scaffold all students so each student has written his name. Remind them that their names carry a very important message. It identifies who they are!

Follow Up

Save these pictures for assessment. Compare to later work. ■

Generating Ideas to Write About

Materials: bowl of colored objects (wood chips, slips of paper, pieces of candy), "What Color is Your Topic?" sharing chart, chart paper, paper, pencils

Prep Step: Prepare a bowl of colored objects. Draw or make a transparency of the sharing chart for display.

Procedure

Pass your bowl of colored objects around. Instruct students to choose only one color from the bowl.

Post the "What Color is Your Topic?" chart (see page 98) on the chalkboard, easel, or overhead. Determine ahead of time which colors you will be including in the bowl, and color the circles on the chart to match.

After each student has chosen a color, explain that every color corresponds to a writing idea. "When you chose a color, you were actually choosing a topic to share and write about!"

Invite any child who chose a yellow object to stand. Have them share their favorite color with the group and then list a few things that are that color.

Next, ask any child who chose red to stand. Have them share a book they enjoy and tell the class why they like that particular book.

Next, have any child who chose orange stand. Have them share a favorite food.

Next, ask any child who chose blue to stand. Have them share a place they like to visit and why.

GOAL

To generate writing topics

Next, have any child who chose purple stand. Have them share a favorite storybook character. If the child knows, have her share the book the character is found in.

Finally, have any child who chose green stand. Have them identify a special person in their life and explain why that person is special.

As the children are sharing, invite conversation about personal connections. Explain that all topics can be worthy of writing pieces, and that writers get their ideas from everywhere: from books, foods, their families, and from each other. Good writers are always looking for ideas to put on paper.

"Keep your ideas in your memory banks, and use them during your quiet writing time."

Follow Up

Give each child a copy of the chart for future reference or simply keep a large one up in the classroom. Change the writing ideas and colors and repeat this lesson when children need new topics for writing. ■

What Color is Your Topic?

Choose a color and tell about:

○ Your favorite color

○ Your favorite book

○ Your favorite food

○ Your favorite place to visit

○ Your favorite storybook character

○ Your favorite special person

Making a Brainstorm List

Materials: magazines, 9"x13" construction paper for each child, glue, scissors, pencils

Prep Step: Collect a class set of magazines, pre-fold a class set of construction paper into six equal sections

Note: If magazines are not available, students can draw their own pictures.

Procedure

Give each student a magazine that contains pictures of food, animals, people, flowers, etc. Invite them to find pictures of items that interest them. These pictures should be of familiar things. They should be able to write a few words or sentences about their pictures.

Demonstrate how a picture of a cat might remind you of your pet cat, Stormy. Cut out the picture and glue it on the upper left-hand square. On the upper-right square write "Stormy, my cat."

Perhaps a picture of a hotdog might remind you of a family picnic. Cut out the picture and glue it on the left-middle square. Then write "I like picnics" in the right-middle square.

Complete the last square with another writing idea. Model using the back if you would like your students to find six ideas from their magazines.

GOAL

To make an individual brainstorm list

Have students cut out their pictures and glue them on a 9"x13" sheet of paper. Pre-fold the paper so that there are six squares on each side. Instruct students to cut their pictures out and glue them on the left-hand squares just as you did. Ask them to write a few words or a sentence that will remind them of why the topic is personal to them.

Identify the list as a "brainstorm list." Explain that each square is a writing idea that is personal only to them. "Sometimes an author can't decide what to write about. A brainstorm list will remind him of some stories that he would like to write." As students complete their brainstorm lists, encourage them to find a partner and share with them.

Follow Up

Repeat this lesson whenever students experience difficulty identifying writing topics. ■

Using Literature to Generate Writing Topics

Materials: Kevin Henkes books, chart paper, markers

Prep Step: Locate the following Kevin Henkes books in your library:

Wemberly Worried; Chrysanthemum; Sheila Rae, the Brave; Owen

Procedure

Tell your class that writers have to look everywhere to get their writing topics. They think about trips they have taken, things they like to do, favorite foods or toys, or their families. These are all great writing ideas.

Share that books are another place writers find ideas to write about. When a writer listens to a picture book, he might make a personal connection to an event, a setting, or a character. The book might remind him of an idea for his own piece. That is why great writers read many books.

Show the covers of each of the Kevin Henkes books listed above. Explain that each of the books holds many writing topics. Give a brief description of what each book is about:

Wemberly Worried
– being afraid of the first day of school

Chrysanthemum
– being made fun of

Sheila Rae, the Brave
– overcoming a fear

Owen
– giving up a childhood blanket

GOAL

To use literature to generate writing topics

Ask for a show of hands: who can relate to any of these themes? Explain that they can use those ideas of Kevin Henkes's as starting places for their own pieces about the same topics.

Follow Up

For the next four days during writer's workshop, read one of the Kevin Henkes books. Discuss the theme and how the characters handle each situation.

Invite students to share their own stories. On chart paper, make a class brainstorm list by recording the writing ideas that emerge from the discussions. You may want to make a simple graphic to go with it. Post this chart so students can use it independently to develop writing topics. ∎

Description

Materials: stickers, chart paper, markers, paper, pencils

Prep Step: None

Procedure

Place a large picture on the chalkboard or easel. Invite your students to look at the picture and tell you what they see. Write their observations on chart paper. For example, if the picture is a kitten you might write these observations:

"I see a kitten. The kitten is gray and white. The kitten is cute and looks like she is smiling. The kitten is tiny. The kitten looks soft."

Now take the picture away and read the class their observations. Ask if they can still picture the kitten in their heads. They should be able to. Explain that a good writer can paint a picture with words just as a painter does with color. Although pictures are important in a book, the reader won't be dependent on a picture if the writer uses descriptive words. Beginning writers need to practice writing descriptive words. Give each child a sticker on a sheet of paper.

GOAL

To model and practice the use of descriptive words

Instruct them to write words that would describe the picture on their sticker. Tell them they can write single descriptive words or complete sentences. Invite them to share with a partner when finished. Instruct them to close their eyes and try to picture the sticker while their partner reads their descriptive words.

Follow Up

One of your writing centers can include papers with stickers so students can continue to practice writing descriptive words. Papers can be stapled together to make a sticker book of descriptions. ■

Leads—Hints, Sounds, Feelings, and Questions

Materials: chart paper, marker, paper, pencils

Prep Step: Prepare a chart about a visit to the park (or any favorite place).

Procedure

Write the following story (or one similar) on a chart and place it on the easel. Read it out loud to the class.

"My favorite place to visit is the park. When I get there I find a comfy spot and lay my blanket on the ground. I stretch out on my back and look at the clouds. I listen to the children playing on the swings and the slide. The sun makes my face feel warm. Sometimes I read a book until I get so sleepy I close my eyes. The park is so relaxing. It is one of my favorite places to visit."

Underline the first sentence. Explain that the first sentence is the lead sentence. It is the sentence that leads the reader into the story. It is just like someone taking the reader's hand and saying, "Come on. Read my piece and see what happens!" The first sentence is very important.

Reread the first sentence on the chart story. Underline it in red. Explain that it lets each reader know the topic of the piece. Now they all know it will be about your favorite place, the park. This kind of lead gives the reader a hint of what the piece will be about. To know why the park is your favorite place they will have to read on. Reread the paragraph. Ask a volunteer to share why the park is your favorite place.

GOAL

To identify and use four types of leads

Next, cross out the first sentence and reread the park piece. Discuss how it sounds without the lead sentence. Reiterate that the lead sentence is very important in a piece. Using a hint is one type of lead. Encourage the class to try this type of lead in one of their pieces.

Follow Up

Other types of leads are sound leads, question leads, or feeling leads. Read the first two sentences of several picture books. Identify the lead. Encourage the class to listen to how it leads the reader into the story. Determine if all the leads are hints about the story. They are not.

Reread your picture book selections and categorize the leads. Repeat the above lesson, replacing a hint lead with one of the other types. Once the four types of leads have been taught, help students identify their leads during individual conferencing. ■

Sequencing Information

Materials: plain paper divided into twelve squares, crayons, pencils

Prep Step: Prepare a large copy of your classroom schedule. Fold a class set of plain paper into twelve squares.

Procedure

Review your classroom schedule. Discuss the different activities that make up the class's day, and talk about why you do them when you do. Ask the following questions:

GOAL

To practice the sequencing of information

✓ Why doesn't the class eat lunch first thing in the morning?

✓ Why do you go outside for recess in the middle of the day?

✓ Why do you put the toys away at the end of the day?

✓ What determines when you do certain activities?

Give each student a sheet of paper folded into twelve squares. Instruct them to draw a picture of one activity they do every day in each square. Ask them to try to sequence them in the order that they happen. When they are finished, invite them to share their schedule with a friend.

Follow Up

Share that sometimes activities are decided by factors we can't control, like time of day. Other activities are determined because of common sense. For example, it wouldn't make sense to eat lunch when they first arrive at school because they have just eaten breakfast. It wouldn't make sense to take a recess break before any work had been done.

Explain that the same concept holds true in writing. When an author is telling a story she should make sure she shares the story in an order that makes sense. Thinking aloud, share this example:

"I want to write a piece about eating an ice cream cone. Should I start with the part about eating the cone, or should I start with getting two scoops of chocolate chip ice cream?" When students determine that getting two scoops of ice cream should come first, write "two scoops" at the top of the chart paper. Then ask what would make the most sense as the next sentence: "The ice cream tastes smooth and creamy" or "Eating the cone is the best part"? Determine that the taste should come next. Write "tastes smooth and creamy" underneath "two scoops."

Then ask what would come next: "I ate the ice cream really fast" or "The cone is the best part"? Write "really fast" underneath the other two examples. Finally, write "cone."

Read what you have written out loud. Share that the order of your ice cream story is important because it wouldn't have made sense to write about eating the cone first before you ever put ice cream on it! Order is important when sharing a story orally or in writing. Now the piece is ready to be written in sentence form. Remind them how important it is to think about the order of the events that make up their piece. ■

Focus

Materials: out-of-focus photograph, chart paper, markers

Prep Step: Obtain a photograph that is out of focus.

Procedure

Show the class an out-of-focus photograph. Discuss how difficult it is to identify the topic of the photograph. Determine that the fuzziness makes it hard to make out the picture and that the picture is out of focus.

Relate this photograph problem to writing. Share that a writing piece out of focus is just as problematic as an out-of-focus photograph. A single piece of writing about several different topics is confusing and fuzzy to the reader. A writer needs to choose one topic and stick to it. The author and the reader should be able to share, in one sentence, the topic of a piece.

Read several pieces of writing to the class. Use pieces from previous years or borrow a few from another teacher. Ask for a volunteer to share—in one sentence—the topic of the piece. If the audience is unable to identify the topic in one sentence, determine why. Reiterate the importance of staying focused on one topic in a piece of writing: if you don't, your reader might not be able to make meaning from your piece.

GOAL

To define focus

Follow Up

Copy the following paragraph. Read it out loud.

"Yesterday I went to the zoo. There were many animals in cages. I like to practice batting in a batting cage. My favorite animal to visit at the zoo is the lion. I also like to visit the beach and the mall. The lion was pacing back and forth on a huge ledge. He looked like he was going to fall but he didn't. One time I fell out of a tree. Lions are very graceful animals. They are also known as 'king of the jungle.' I don't really know any kings. The zoo is a great place to see a lion."

Determine the focus of the paragraph. Eliminate the sentences that are not focused. Reread the paragraph and discuss how it is different. Discuss how the second piece is focused and the first piece isn't. ■

Endings—Feelings, Reworded Beginnings, and Questions

Materials: chart story, sentence strips, markers

Prep Step: Write a story about school on a sheet of chart paper.

Procedure

Read your chart-paper story as a class.

"I like going to kindergarten. I like to play with blocks. I build trains and airplanes with yellow and green blocks. I paint rainbows on the easel. I use every color. Housekeeping is fun, too. I like to wear the apple apron and set the table."

Ask the class for feedback about the chart story. Determine if it seems to be missing something. (It is missing an ending.) Explain that all good pieces of writing have an ending. An author doesn't just write "the end." He can let his reader know his piece is finished in several different ways.

Explain that one way an author lets a reader know he is finished is by sharing a feeling. Reread the chart story. Together think of a feeling word to describe what the author thinks about school. On a sentence strip write, "I like kindergarten." Tape it at the end of the story. Reread the entire story with the ending. Discuss the difference between the story with an ending and the story without ending.

GOAL

To identify and use three types of endings

Follow Up

The next day, reread your chart-paper story again. Tell your students that besides ending the piece with a feeling, there are two other ways you could end it: rewording the beginning and asking a question.

Explain that you are going to try to reword the beginning of your piece. On a sentence strip, write "Kindergarten is one of my favorite places to go." Tape it underneath the other sentence strip. Reread the story with the new ending.

Finally, on a differently colored sentence strip write, "Do you like going to kindergarten?" Explain this is a question ending. Add it to the chart and reread the story with the question ending.

Explain that all the endings are fine. It is up to the writer to choose which kind of ending fits his story. However, remind your students that every writing piece needs to have an ending.

Read different endings from well-known picture books. Determine the type of endings the authors have used. ∎

Describing a Setting

Materials: *Night Tree*, chart paper, markers, paper, pencils

Prep Step: Obtain a copy of *Night Tree* by Eve Bunting

Procedure

Ask a few students to describe what the classroom looks like. Next, ask a few students to describe what their bedrooms at home look like.

As a class, discuss which room is easier to picture in your minds: the classroom or the bedrooms? The classroom is, because the students who described the classroom could use their eyes to look at details as they reported them. When the students described their bedrooms at home, they had to rely on their memories, and may not have given all the details they could have.

Explain that writers have to use specific details to create a "setting"—the place where the story is happening. Sometimes an author will use a picture to create the setting, or sometimes she will use words. However, it is always important for the author to construct a vivid setting at the beginning of the piece, so the reader can become involved in the action. When readers can picture the place where the action is occurring, it is easier to "watch" the action unfold.

> ### GOAL
> **To demonstrate how writers use specific details to create a setting**

Introduce *Night Tree* by Eve Bunting. Show your students the cover of the book and read the title. Explain that the story shares one family's Christmas tradition. Every year, they go into the woods and decorate a tree with edible treats for the animals. Ask your students to listen for the specific details the author uses to allow us, the readers, to picture the woods on a winter night.

Now read the book aloud. Give each student a sheet of paper and crayons. Have them draw the setting of the story. Share the pictures and determine why each student drew a forest. The details in the book helped them all to picture the setting. Encourage them to try creating a setting in every writing piece.

Follow Up

Before writing, ask students to draw pictures of the setting their piece is going to take place in. Then have them begin composing their pieces. Discuss whether it was easier to write when the setting was drawn first. The strategy of drawing the setting first may help reluctant writers. ∎

Using Transition Words

Materials: transition words on index cards, chart paper, marker, bread, peanut butter, jelly, butter knife

Prep Step: Write the following words on index cards: "first," "next," "then," "finally." Bring in supplies needed to make a peanut butter and jelly sandwich.

Procedure

Make a peanut butter and jelly sandwich in front of the class. Describe the process as you make the sandwich, explaining each step of what you are doing. When you are finished, invite the children to repeat the steps of the procedure back to you out loud. "Remember, it is important to put the steps in order of what you did first, what you did second, etc." Make sure that the students understand how important order is.

Next, explain that you are going to write the steps for making a peanut butter and jelly sandwich so you don't forget them. Show the class your index cards with the transition words on them. Read each one. Explain that those words are "transition words." They will help keep the directions for making a peanut butter and jelly clear and in the right order. They help move a piece of writing forward so that it doesn't get stuck in one place.

GOAL

To demonstrate how transition words help move a piece of writing forward

Pass out the transition word cards to five students. Ask them to stand in front of the class in this order: first, next, then, finally. Retell the directions again emphasizing the transition words.

Follow Up

Write the directions for making a peanut butter and jelly sandwich on a sheet of chart paper. Invite students to bring the transition word cards to the easel and tape them beside the correct sentence. This could be repeated to allow all students an opportunity to manipulate a transition word. ■

Beginning, Middle, End

Materials: chart paper with drawn snowman, marker

Prep Step: Draw a snowman on a large sheet of chart paper.

Procedure

Orally share a winter story with your students. For example:

"Winter is my favorite season because I love to play in the snow. I build a snowman with a fat tummy. I use rocks for his eyes and a stick for his mouth. I make snowballs and throw them at my brother. We lie on the ground and make snow angels. Winter is so much fun. I never want it to end."

Ask if they could tell which part was the beginning. Ask for a volunteer to identify it. Write "Winter is my favorite season because I love to play in the snow" inside the head of the snowman on the chart.

Ask for a volunteer to retell the middle of the piece. Write, "I build a snowman with a fat tummy. I use rocks for his eyes and a stick for his mouth. I make snowballs and throw them at my brother. We lie on the ground and make snow angels," in the middle circle of the snowman.

GOAL

To identify the beginning, middle, and end of a piece

Ask a third volunteer to identify the ending. Write "Winter is so much fun. I never want it to end" in the last circle of the snowman.

Explain that all stories should have a clear beginning, middle, and end. Ask if they were able to identify those parts in your story. If they think about the parts of a snowman, they will always remember to include a beginning, a middle, and an end when they are writing. Share that the beginning is the lead-in to the piece, the middle is the biggest part of the piece, and the end wraps it all up. "All of your writing pieces should have all three parts! Think about each part before you begin writing."

Follow Up

Repeat this lesson using different graphics to emphasize the three parts of a story. ∎

Craft Mini-Lessons

Target Skills Addressed

- details
- active verbs
- alliteration
- elaboration
- similes
- comparing/contrasting
- description
- moving from general to specific
- varied sentences

Using Details in Writing

Materials: basket of plastic fruit or vegetables, chart paper, blank paper, crayons, pencil

Prep Step: None

Procedure

Choose a piece of fruit from the basket and show it to the class. Invite them to share details about the piece of fruit with a partner. Then gather the whole group together and share their observations. Record their details on a sheet of chart paper.

Go over each word of their descriptions and discuss what kind of word it is. It might be a color word, a size word, a texture word, or a use for the fruit. Explain that the words recorded are details about the piece of fruit. Those details would help the reader picture the fruit in their minds even though they weren't holding it in their hands.

Repeat the procedure with another piece of fruit.

Next, reverse the procedure. Write words describing a fruit on the chart, and have a volunteer choose which fruit it is from the basket. (Make sure the correct fruit was chosen.) Explain that the detail words that you wrote on the chart helped them to see the fruit in their heads even though you didn't say the name of the fruit. This is why they were able to choose the correct fruit.

> **GOAL**
>
> *To demonstrate how details help create a picture in a reader's mind*

Remind students that details are important words to use in their writing. When they use words that tell the color, size, shape, texture or use their readers will have a better understanding of their piece. Encourage them to try at least one detail word in a sentence they are writing during writer's workshop.

Follow Up

Determine a class topic like pets, candy, sports, etc. Use student partners. One partner shares details about a specific item pertaining to that topic. The other partner draws a picture. ■

Active Verbs

Materials: chart paper, index cards, glitter glue, markers, paper, pencils

Prep Step: None

Procedure

Ask students to come to the gathering area and sit in a circle. Choose one student and instruct him to "go" around the circle. As the child moves around the circle, record the action word that identifies his movement. For example, if the child walks around the circle, record the word "walk" on a piece of chart paper. Remember to think aloud and segment sounds as you write.

Choose another child to move around the circle in a different way. Record their action. Repeat the procedure until you have a long list of ways the students were able to move around the circle.

Read the list with your students. Have the students pantomime the action as you read. Determine that people move in many ways. Explain that when a writer wants his reader to see an action she must use a specific word that shows the action. That way the reader can see the character move through the writer's words. If a sentence simply reads "I went to the park," the reader can't picture the action. How did the writer get to the park? Did he run to the park? Did he ride his bike or maybe skip? Active verbs provide the action. Strong sentences have strong active verbs. Invite students to try writing some action words in their journals.

GOAL

To practice using specific words to show action

Follow Up

Cut the individual action words from the class-made list. For subsequent mini-lessons, choose one of the words and model how to write a sentence using it. Underline the action. Give each child a word and an index card. Instruct each child to draw a picture that would illustrate their word. Glue these index cards to a large sheet and display it in the room to use as a resource. ■

CRAFT MINI-LESSON 3

Color Words

Materials: paint-store sample chips, chart paper, paper, pencils

Prep Step: obtain paint chips from a paint store

Procedure

Ask your students to picture a truck in their minds. Get volunteers to share what color truck they were thinking of. Observe that not everyone was thinking of the same color truck. "In order for everyone to think of the same color truck, we would need to know what color to think of. Let's try it again. Let's all picture a red truck in our minds." Repeat the procedure with a green truck, then pink, etc. Make note that now everyone is seeing the same color because you shared the color word.

Explain that writers have to use color words when they are writing so their reader can see the colors in their heads.

Next, brainstorm a list of colors and make a chart. Choose one color at a time and orally list some items that would be that color. Make note that some items come in a variety of colors. For example, if a writer mentions a banana in her piece, most readers will probably picture the banana as being yellow, since bananas are usually yellow. But apples can be red, yellow, or green.

The writer will have to use a color word to help the reader see the apple as the writer does. Encourage your young writers to include color words in their sentences during writer's workshop. If your students' are not writing sentences yet, encourage them to make a list of color words along with items that are that color.

GOAL

To practice using color words as a detail

Follow Up

A future writer's workshop might include looking at paint chips from a hardware or discount store. Those chips have interesting names for colors and are fun to use in writing. Students can insert those color words into their own sentences using words like "laser lemon yellow" instead of just yellow. ∎

Translation of Temporary Spelling

The light brown desert snake with laser lemon fangs at the top of his head. When his tongue's out he is mad. When he shakes his chestnut brown rattle he is also mad. One way is when he sticks his tongue out and the other way is when he shakes his rattle.

Alliteration

Materials: chart paper, marker, index cards with student names, paper, pencil

Prep Step: Write your students' names on a sheet of chart paper.

Procedure

Display a list of student names on a chart. Have each student find their name and identify its first letter.

Next brainstorm a list of action words and record them on chart paper. Read each one to try to match the beginning sounds of each name to an action word. For example, "Julie jumps" or "Willie walks." Add the action word to the name chart. "Look again at the beginning sounds. They are the same."

Explain that writers sometimes deliberately use words that start with the same sound as another word-starting sound in a sentence. "This is a writer's technique called 'alliteration.' Starting their words this way makes the sentence fun to read and provides rhythm to the words."

GOAL

To model how to deliberately use words that start with the same sound in a sentence

Go over the class-made chart and read the two-word sentences. Point out that you could add more detail to the sentences by using more alliteration. Model with a couple of examples from the chart. For example, "Willie walks wiggly." Share however, that the sentence must make sense for it to be a truly alliterative sentence.

Challenge the class to use their names in a sentence along with an action that starts with the same sound. If they want to use the example made in class, encourage them to add a new word.

Follow Up

See the bibliography for good examples of alliteration in literature. ■

Unpacking a Heavy Sentence

Materials: small suitcase or backpack, reprinted sentence strips, tape

Prep Step: Pre-print sentence strips

Procedure

Show your class a small suitcase. Ask if anyone has ever packed a suitcase for a trip. Get a volunteer to share what kinds of things went into their suitcase. "That's a lot of stuff! Was it heavy? Did it ever get too heavy to carry?"

Explain that writers also do some packing when they compose sentences. Sentences are like suitcases that carry the writer's details. Unfortunately, sometimes a writer thinks a sentence can carry more detail than it really can. Just like an over-packed suitcase, sentences can get too heavy. When this happens the reader misses important details that help tell the story.

Write this sentence on a chart or chalkboard: "The birthday party was fun." Read the sentence together. Explain that the sentence is "heavy"—there are too many details packed into it for it to be easy to carry all at once. As a class, talk about all the things that could have happened at the party. "Too bad we don't know about all the exciting things that did happen. But all the party's details are packed into this one sentence, and it's too heavy to carry."

Have these sentences pre-printed on sentence strips and placed inside the suitcase ahead of time:

First we played Pin the Tail on the Donkey.

Then we played Musical Chairs.

After that, we decorated our own cupcakes with icing and sprinkles.

Then we ate them.

Finally, Susie opened her presents.

GOAL

To demonstrate how to create a piece from a heavy sentence

Unpack the suitcase by pulling the strips out one at a time. At this point, the order isn't important. Tape the sentences on the easel or chalkboard under the heavy sentence ("The birthday party was fun"). Reread all the sentences together. Then place them in an order that would make sense.

Explain that now that the sentence is unpacked, it is easy to understand why the birthday party was fun. "All those details were important and shouldn't be hidden inside one sentence."

This lesson could be repeated for future writer's workshops using these "packed" sentences:

My sister is funny.

I like school.

My mom is nice.

Soccer is my favorite sport.

Follow Up

These sentence strips can also be used to teach or review the importance of transition words. Point out the transition words on the sentence strips and identify the role that they play in understanding how the sentences work together.

The lesson can also be used to review leads and endings, and beginning, middle, and end. Identify the lead sentence ("The birthday party was fun") as the beginning of the piece. Move on to identify the next five sentences as the middle of the piece. Point out that there is not an ending. Add an ending by either rewording the beginning, asking a question, or sharing a feeling. ■

Connecting Sentences Using "And"

Materials: sentence strips, chart paper, markers

Prep Step: Create several simple list sentences on sentence strips. For example:

I like dogs.
I like cats.
I like babies.
I like chocolate ice cream.
I like vanilla ice cream.

Procedure

Invite the class to read the pre-written sentences with you. Explain that they are good sentences for a kindergartner. They are all readable and make sense. "But there is a way they could be made better. Maybe we could put some of these sentences together to make them more interesting for the reader." The sentences become longer and don't sound like the lists of beginning writers.

Read the first two sentences out loud. Ask for a volunteer to share how the word "and" could connect those two sentences so that it becomes one that reads, "I like dogs and cats." Ask if there are two other sentences that could go together. Lead the class to see that "I like chocolate and vanilla ice cream" makes sense as a single sentence. Explore adding one of the other sentence strips to "I like babies." Nothing really goes with that sentence so it would stand alone.

Try the procedure again with "I can run. I can jump. I can laugh. I can cry." Write the two new sentences on chart paper. "I can run and jump. I can laugh and cry."

> ### GOAL
>
> *To practice connecting sentences with the word "and"*

Give each student a sentence strip and ask them to write one sentence about something they like. Then have them find a partner. As a team, they should rewrite their two individual sentences into one. Remind students to try this in their own writing.

Follow-up

When students are first beginning to put their thoughts on paper, they often use the structure of a list sentence. For example, "I like..." or "I can..." are common for beginning writers. If students have written list sentences previously, these could be used for extended practice in combining sentences. Invite them to revise some list sentences from their journals by connecting them using the word "and." ■

General to Specific Words

Materials: blank paper, crayons, chart, paper, pencils
Prep Step: Draw two-columns on a sheet of chart paper.

Procedure

Emergent writers often use very general terms in their beginning pieces. They might write "I like my pet" instead of the more specific "I like my dog." It is important to show them the difference between general topics and specific nouns and verbs. Specific words make a sentence stronger.

Have a general-to-specific hunt in your classroom. On a large sheet of chart paper, draw a simple two-column chart. Write the word "girl" three times in the left-hand column. Then ask your students to orally share names of girls in the class. Choose three names. Write these in the right-hand column of the chart, opposite of each "girl."

Point out how specific the names are, and how general the word "girl" is. "The real names are more specific because they give us a face to put with the word 'girl.' Now we can all picture the 'girl' because we know what her name is."

Write this sentence at the bottom of the chart. "I like my friend." Now write, "I like Cindy." Ask which uses a specific word that paints a clearer picture for the reader.

GOAL

To model how to use specific words to communicate in writing

Repeat the procedure with the words "went" and "toys." Reiterate that it is always better to use the specific word over the general category. The ability to categorize information from general-to-specific is an important skill in all academic areas. Encourage the class to pick the most specific words they can when they write. Remind them to tell their reader exactly who or what they mean.

Follow Up

Repeat the lesson using the general-to-specific box diagram and different words. ∎

Similes Using Color Words

Materials: box of crayons, chart paper, plain paper, markers

Prep Step: None

Procedure

Share with the class a box of sixty-four crayons. Explain that there are many colors in the world to enjoy. Read a few of the crayon names out loud. Share that colors are just as important to writers as they are to artists. "Sometimes a writer will use a color word and compare it to something else the same color so that the reader will imagine just the right picture."

Use one crayon as an example. Hold up a blue. Everyone should close their eyes and think of something blue. Invite the class to share their thoughts. Record a few on a chart under the heading "Blue." Some examples might be "the sky," "water," "blueberries," or "jeans."

Ask for a volunteer who has blue eyes to stand up. Write a sentence that contains a simile: "Joyce's eyes are as blue as blueberries." Make note that you compared Joyce's eyes to blueberries because both are really blue.

Ask for a volunteer to share another sentence you could write about Joyce's eyes. This time compare them to something else that is blue. Record that sentence. Repeat the procedure as many times as you like and then move to another color.

GOAL

To practice writing similes using color words

Follow Up

As an extension activity, divide the class into small groups and then assign each group a color by passing out crayons. Have each group brainstorm a list of items that are the color of their crayon.

Group members should take turns being the recorder that writes the group's list on the chart. Encourage them to help each other segment sounds and write a letter for each sound that they hear in the word.

Call the groups back to the gathering area to share their color lists. These lists could then be used to practice similes orally, and to write similes comparing two items. For example: "The dog was as brown as a stick" or "The cloud was as white as snow."

Leave the box of crayons in a writing center for the students to read and write color words at their leisure. ■

Specific Word Choice

Materials: chart paper, markers, paper, pencils

Prep Step: None

Procedure

Gather the class together in front of the easel. Share the scenario of a kindergartner who continually leaves her lunch box at school. Every day before school her mother reminds her to bring it home. Every day after school her mother asks her if she remembered it. For three days straight she forgets. Ask the class how the mother would be feeling. Accept all responses but choose "mad" to write on the far left-hand side of a large sheet of chart paper.

Then share the scenario of the same little girl playing catch in the house with her brother. Her mother reminds her that playing ball is for outside and to stop throwing the ball inside. The little girl throws the ball to her brother one more time and breaks her mother's favorite lamp. Ask how the mother would be feeling now. Accept all responses but focus on the word "furious." Lead the class in a discussion about which feeling is stronger: "furious" or "mad." Write "furious" on the far right hand side of the chart.

Finally share the scenario of the same girl fighting and fighting with her brother. Again, her mother asks her to stop but she continues picking on her brother. Ask how mom is feeling now. Is she more than mad? Is she less than furious? Suggest the word, "angry." Ask where that word would go on the chart. Place it between "mad" and "furious."

Share with the class that we have many words in our language that mean somewhat the same thing. The mother in each of the scenarios was upset about her daughter's behavior. But her feelings were stronger in the case of the lamp than in the case of the lunch box.

> **GOAL**
>
> *To model choosing words that portray exact feelings*

When writing, it is the job of the author to choose a word that portrays an exact feeling. The word "mad" just isn't strong enough to let the reader know how the mother felt about her broken lamp. "Furious" would be a better choice. Demonstrate how these words can be used in a sentence:

My mom was mad when I forgot my lunch box.

My mom gets angry when I fight with my brother.

My mom was furious when I broke her favorite lamp.

Brainstorm other words that could be used in writing to portray anger. Place these words on the continuum. Keep this chart visible for students to use during quiet writing. Encourage students to think carefully about their word choices as they are writing.

Of course, developing vocabulary in young children is a continual process. Some children may have a difficult time thinking of a word that means somewhat the same thing as another word. As their vocabulary grows the task will become easier. Meanwhile, they will benefit from hearing other students or the teacher supply synonyms.

Follow Up

This mini-lesson could be repeated using a variety of words. Other words that work well for building continuums of feeling are "happy," "funny," "big," "little," or "pretty." ∎

Elaboration

Materials: chart paper, markers

Prep Step: None

Procedure

Gather your students together on the floor in a circle. Explain that they are going to practice a writing skill called "elaboration." "Elaboration is about giving the reader more information."

Explain that you will start with a simple two- or three-word sentence. Then the person to your right will add a word or phrase to it. The addition can be made anywhere in the sentence, but the sentence must still make sense.

The next person must repeat the sentence and add another word or phrase, and so on. Continue as far around the circle as you can. Once the sentence becomes incoherent, stop. As the sentence grows, record it on your white board or on a large sheet of chart paper. Students can help each other remember the sentence as it grows.

Here are some example "finished" sentences:

> The dolphin swims.
> The dolphin swims fast.
> The little dolphin swims fast.
> The pretty little dolphin swims fast.
> The pretty little gray dolphin swims fast.
> The pretty little gray dolphin swims fast in the water.
> The pretty little gray dolphin swims fast in the cool water.
> The pretty little gray dolphin swims fast as lightning in the cool water.

GOAL

To practice giving more information through elaboration

Follow Up

After practicing orally, future mini-lessons could include writing elaborated sentences as a group, or individually during quiet writing.

Here are some additional "starter" sentences:

The man ran.	The baby cries.
The girl swims.	The rain falls.
The boy plays.	My sister reads. ■

Linking Sentences for Elaboration

Materials: sentence strips, markers, paper, pencils

Prep Step: Gather sentence strips in five different colors.

Procedure

Ask one child to stand up and mention a person, place, or thing. "Pizza," they might say. Have them use their word in a sentence: "I like pizza." Underline their original word, the one that identified their person, place, or thing. "Let's call this 'the Big Idea.'" (The first few times you practice linking sentences you might want to provide the word and the sentence.)

Write the Big Idea sentence on a pink sentence strip. Ask the child to hold it so it's visible to everyone. Read the sentence as a class.

Next, ask the class to think about an idea that would link to that first sentence. Encourage students to think about the underlined word ("pizza"), and encourage them to make up a new sentence about it. Invite a volunteer to share a linking sentence. "The cheese is the best part," they might say. Write it on a green sentence strip. Have the second volunteer stand next to the first volunteer and display the topic-sentence strip. Read both sentence strips aloud. "The first sentence is the Big Idea. This new sentence is the topic sentence." Underline the most important word on the topic-sentence strip (in this case, "cheese"). "So our Big Idea is 'pizza,' but our specific topic is 'cheese.'"

Explain that the next sentence (the third sentence) should give some detail or link to the underlined word in the topic sentence. Ask for a volunteer to share a detail sentence that links to "cheese." "The cheese is steamy and hot" would be an appropriate link. Write this detail sentence

GOAL

To practice elaboration by linking sentences

on a blue sentence strip. Have the third volunteer stand next to the other two students holding sentence strips. Read them all aloud.

Ask for another sentence that would link on to sentence three. Tell them that another detail about cheese would be the best link. "The cheese hangs like long pieces of silly string off my plate" would be a detail linking sentence. Write this detail sentence on another blue sentence strip and have the fourth volunteer stand in line with the other three. Read all the sentences aloud.

Ask for one more linking detail sentence. Remind them that you're looking for another detail about cheese. "If I'm not careful, the cheese will burn the roof of my mouth" could be the third detail sentence. Write it another blue sentence strip. Ask the volunteer to stand with the other sentences. Read all the sentences aloud.

Finally, ask for a linking sentence that would remind the reader of the topic and wrap up the paragraph. For example: "Pizza is my favorite food." Write this sentence on an orange sentence strip. It will be the ending. Have a volunteer stand with the rest of the sentences. Read all the sentences together.

Return to the beginning of the line and ask for a sentence that will lead the reader into the Big Idea. Remind students to use a sound word, a hint, a question, or a feeling to hook the reader. "Do you have a favorite food?" would be an example of a question lead. Write this sentence on a yellow sentence strip. Have a volunteer hold this strip in front of all the other sentences.

You now have a complete paragraph with all sentences linked together. The entire paragraph looks like this:

(yellow sentence strip) Do you have a favorite food? (Question Lead)

(pink sentence strip) I like pizza. (Big Idea)

(green sentence strip) The cheese part is the best. (Topic Sentence)

(blue sentence strip) The cheese is steamy and hot. (Detail Sentence)

(blue sentence strip) The cheese hangs like long pieces of silly string off my plate. (Detail Sentence)

(blue sentence strip) If I'm not careful, the cheese will burn the roof of my mouth. (Detail Sentence)

(orange sentence strip) Pizza is my favorite food. (Ending)

To emphasize the importance of the different types of sentences have the students holding certain colors step out of the paragraph line. For example, have all the detail sentences step out. Read their sentences. The paragraph sounds incomplete.

Hang the sentence strips in a chain in your classroom as a reminder for your students to link their sentences together.

Follow Up

Encourage students to try their own linking sentences in small groups. This activity could also be used as a homework activity. Repeat this mini-lesson many times throughout the year. ∎

> The beach is fun to visit.
> I like to make sand casts
> I will make a door.
> I will shoop the sand down to
> make a door I put glitr on it
> My mom pacs pynut
> budr and jele
> samwuchis. We sat on
> toats taws. and
> weat them. Yum yum!
> Naw yaa no abawt
> the beach.

<table>
<tr><td>Translation of Temporary Spelling</td></tr>
<tr><td>The beach is fun to visit. I like to make sandcastles. I will make a door. I will scoop the sand down to make a door. I put glitter on it. My mom packs peanut butter and jelly sandwiches. We sat on towels and we ate them. Yum, yum! Now you know about the beach.</td></tr>
</table>

Inserting Information

Materials: skinny orange markers, chart paper, marker, paper, pencil

Prep Step: Write a simple narrative on a sheet of chart paper. Gather enough orange markers for your class to each have one.

Procedure

Prewrite a simple narrative on chart paper. Read the piece with your students. Invite any questions they have about it. Think out loud as you answer their questions. Share that you would like to add some information to your piece that answers some of their questions. This would make your piece clearer.

Present the problem that you don't want to rewrite your entire piece. Most of your piece is good. But you want to make the parts that aren't clear as good as the rest. Share that you know a writer's strategy that could help you. It is called "using a caret."

Invite volunteers to share what they think a caret might be. Accept all responses. Write the word "caret." Talk about how it sounds like another word. Then define "caret" as "a symbol used by writers to insert information." Using an orange marker, write the caret symbol ("^") on the chart underneath your piece.

GOAL

To demonstrate how to use a caret to insert information

Return to your writing piece. Choose a place in the piece where information needs to be inserted. Make a caret ^ and insert the information in the appropriate place. "Sometimes writers forget a word or an entire sentence. A caret allows them to put that information into their piece without erasing or rewriting. Carets are useful for all types of writing."

As a group, practice segmenting sounds and writing simple sentences. As you are dictating a sentence to your students, purposely leave out a word. Pass out the orange markers. Insert the word together using a caret.

An example of the use of a caret:

My sister is funny.

   little
My ^ sister is funny. ■

Describing Feelings Using the Five Senses

Materials: chart paper, markers, paper, pencils

Prep Step: None

Procedure

Talk to your students about all the things they can write about. Remind them how important it is for them to be as specific as possible when describing different things in their writing. "When you can see and touch the objects you're describing, you can use your five senses to tell what the object felt like, or looked like, tasted like, etc." (Review the five senses.)

"But there are times when an author wants to write about feelings. These feelings can be more difficult to paint with words because you can't see, hear, touch, taste or smell them. But a writer can compare feelings to the five senses. This helps the reader to understand the feelings of the writer."

Brainstorm a list of feelings like love, sadness, loneliness, happiness, etc. Choose one and plug it into the comparison stems found below. Orally discuss appropriate responses to the stem. An example might be "Love sounds like singing" or "Love sounds like laughter." Construct a chart using all the senses.

_____ sounds like_____

_____ looks like_____

_____ tastes like_____

_____ smells like_____

_____ feels like_____

GOAL

To practice describing feelings using the five senses

Follow Up

Repeat this activity with different topics. Some ideas to use are "seasons," "holidays," "families," or "friends." The stems can be pre-printed or written independently. ■

Compare/Contrast

Materials: animal pictures, index cards, chart paper, tape, markers

Prep Step: Find two pictures—one each of different animals.

Procedure

Share two animal pictures. Tape them to the top of a large sheet of chart paper, one across from the other. Discuss the attributes of each animal. Choose four attributes and write them underneath each picture. Besides looks, attributes could be habitat, eating habits, etc. For example:

cat	dog
animal	animal
black	brown
four legs	four legs
pet	pet

Highlight the attributes that are the same in red. Highlight the ones that are different in blue. Point out that the red words are ways the dog and cat are alike. The blue words are ways in which they are different.

Tape two new pictures to the chart. Give each student four index cards. Choose one of the animals and model how to write its name on one of the index cards. Discuss some attributes of that animal. Make a list under it. Ask students to choose three of those attributes and write one on each of the remaining index cards. (They can choose words off the chart or write one not mentioned.) Distribute four more index cards and repeat the process with the other animal.

> ### GOAL
>
> *To use compare and contrast to write clear pictures for a reader*

Next, have students place all their cards on the floor in front of them. Instruct them to lay out their cards in a chart, with the animal's name at the top and the cards with the attributes underneath. They should have two rows of index cards. Have them look for words that match. Matches determine ways the two animals are alike. The other words determine ways the animals are different.

Follow Up

An extension of this lesson would be to string the cards together to make two mobiles. Place the cards for similar attributes in the same spot in each mobile.

Another extension would be to write sentences comparing and contrasting two animals or objects using these stems:

A _____ and a _____ are alike because they are both _____.

A _____ and a _____ are different because they are _____.

The stem sentences could be pre-printed to practice the structure of compare/contrast sentences. ∎

Writing a Letter

Materials: *Dear Mr. Blueberry*, chart paper, markers, structured stationary

Prep Step: Read *Dear Mr. Blueberry* by Simon James to the class before this lesson. Copy a class set of the structured stationary that is included with this lesson.

Procedure

With your class, brainstorm a list of people they might want to send a letter to. The list may include parents, grandparents, aunts and uncles, cousins, siblings, friends, the principal, the media specialist, etc.

Choose a person the class would like to send a letter to. Model how to write a letter by writing one together on chart paper. Include a greeting, the body or message, and a closing. Reread the letter together. Define each part for the class and point it out in the letter. Fold it and put it in a large envelope for delivery.

GOAL

To model and practice writing a letter that includes a greeting, body, and closing

Follow Up

Invite each student to choose a person they would like to send a letter to. Supply each child with a sheet of structured stationery. Refer back to Mr. Blueberry to identify the types of information they would want to include in a letter. Review the parts of a letter using the structured stationery.

Instruct students to write their letters. Collect each child's letter and send it home in a blank envelope. Request that parents help them address and mail their letter. Encourage students to bring in and share letters they receive in response. ■

Dear _____

Love,

_____

Literature List

Title	Author	Operational Mini-Lessons	Print Awareness Mini-Lessons	Foundational Mini-Lessons	Craft Mini-Lessons	Also good for modeling
A Fly in the Sky*	Kristen Joy Pratt		X	X		non-fiction
A Tree Can Be...*	Judy Nayer		X			diagrams
A Whale Is Not A Fish*	Melvin Berger		X			comparing and contrasting
Alexander and the No Good, Horrible, Very Bad Day	Judith Viorst			X		organizing
All About Turtles*	Jim Arnosky		X			organization
Amazing Snakes*	Alexandra Parsons		X			text/illustrations
Amelia Hits the Road	Marissa Moss			X		diaries
An Egg is An Egg	Nicki Weiss		X			repeating lines
Begin at the Beginning	Amy Schwartz	X				getting started
Big Red Apple	Tony Johnston		X			cause/effect
Book! Book! Book!	Deborah Bruss		X	X		sound words
Bugs*	Nancy Winslow Parker		X			diagrams
Building a House*	Byron Barton		X			sequencing
Butterflies Fly*	Yvonne Winer			X		strong verbs
Cat and Dog at School	Rozanne Williams	X			X	looks/sounds like
Cat's Colors	Jane Cabrera		X			questions
Charolotte's Web	E. B. White		X			sensory writing
Dear Mr. Blueberry	Simon James		X	X		letter writing
Everybody Needs a Rock	Byrd Baylor		X	X	X	building a rubric
Feathers For Lunch	Lois Ehlert		X			labels
Five Little Monkeys	Eileen Christelow		X			strong verbs
Flicker Flash	Joan Graham		X	X		poetry, details
Grandad Bill's Song	Jane Yolen		X		X	questions and answers
Grandpa Never Lies	Ralph Fletcher		X			writing ideas
Gray Fox*	Jonathan London		X			description
Have You Seen Bugs?*	Joanne Oppenheim		X	X		leads, alliteration
How Does the Wind Walk?*	Nancy Carlstrom			X		questions
How to Lose All Your Friends	Nancy Carlson		X			lists
"I Can't" said the Ant	Polly Cameron	X			X	working together
I Love Animals	Flora McDonnell		X			vignettes
I Love You the Purplest	Barbara Joosse		X	X		description
I Spy Series	Jean Marzollo		X			riddles
I Wonder Why*	Lois Rock				X	question marks
If I Were in Charge of the World	Judith Viorst		X			poetry, innovation
If You Take A Mouse	Laura Numeroff			X		circular endings
In November*	Cynthia Rylant		X	X		innovation, details

*denotes non-fiction

Literature List

Title	Author	Operational Mini-Lessons	Print Awareness Mini-Lessons	Foundational Mini-Lessons	Craft Mini-Lessons	Also good for modeling
Jessica	Kevin Henkes		X			writing ideas
Junie B. Jones Series	Barbara Parke		X	X	X	word play
Just My Friend and Me	Mercer Mayer		X		X	writing ideas
Koala Lou	Mem Fox		X			writing ideas
Letters From Felix	Annette Langen	X	X		X	letter writing
Mrs. Wishy Washy	Joy Cowley		X			
My Little Island	Frane Lessac		X			description
My Mom is Excellent*	Nick Butterworth		X			elaboration
My Mother's Hands	Sheila McGraw		X			repeating lines
Night Tree	Eve Bunting		X	X		setting
Now What Can I Do?	Margaret Bridges		X			conversations
On the Same Day in March*	Marilyn Singer		X			comparing and contrasting
Over in the Meadow	Paul Galdone				X	dialogue
Right Outside My Window*	Mary Ann Hoberman		X			innovation
School Days	B.G. Hennessy		X		X	lists
School Supplies	Lee Bennett Hopkins		X	X	X	poetry, use of space
Silver Seeds*	Paul Paolilli		X	X		poetry, details
Sky Tree*	Thomas Locker		X	X	X	oral language
Sleep Little One, Sleep	Marion Bauer			X		verbs
Some Smug Slug	Pamela Duncan			X		alliteration
Spots	Laura Regan			X		active verbs
That's Good, That's Bad	Margery Cuyler		X		X	innovation, punctuation
The Everything Book*	Denise Fleming		X		X	labels
The Lotus Seed	Sherry Garland		X	X		voice
The Night Before Kindergarten	Natasha Wing	X	X		X	innovation
The Storm Book	Charollote Zolotow			X		showing not telling
The Sunsets of Miss Olivia Wiggins	Lester Laminack		X			endings
The Ticky Tacky Doll	Cynthia Rylant		X	X		
Things That Are Most	Judi Barrett		X			lists
Tough Boris	Mem Fox		X			seesaw text
Whales*	Cynthia Rylant			X		word choice
What Do Authors Do?	Eileen Christelow	X	X	X	X	non-fiction
What Do Writers Do?	Susan Canizares	X				communication
When Winter Comes*	Robert Maas		X			non-fiction
Who Hoots?	Katie Davis		X			questions and answers
With Love, Little Red Hen	Alma Flor Ada		X			letter writing
Your First Step	Henry Sorensen			X		setting

*denotes non-fiction

Bibliography of Recommended Professional Literature

Avery, Carol. ...*And with a Light Touch*. Portsmouth, NH: Heinemann,1993, 2000.

Calkins, Lucy McCormick. *The Art of Teaching Reading*. Portsmouth NH: Heinemann, 2000.

Calkins, Lucy McCormick. *The Art of Teaching Writing*. Portsmouth NH: Heinemann, 1986, 1994.

Camborne, Briane. *The Whole Story: Natural Learning and the Acquisition of Literacy in the Classroom*. Aukland, NZ: Ashton Scholastic, 1993.

Clay, Marie M. *An Observation Survey of Early Literacy Achievement*. Portsmouth NH: Heinemann, 1993.

Dierking, Connie Campbell and Susan Anderson McElveen. *Teaching Writing Skills with Children's Literature*. Gainesville, FL: Maupin House, 1998.

Fletcher, Ralph. *What a Writer Needs*. Portsmouth, NH: Heinemann, 1993.

Freeman, Marcia S. *Teaching the Youngest Writer: A Practical Guide*. Gainesville, FL: Maupin House, 1998.

Freeman, Marcia S. *Non-fiction Writing Strategies: Using Science Big Books as Models*. Gainesville, FL: Maupin House, 2001.

Hansen, Jane. *When Writers Read*. Portsmouth, NH: Heinemann, 1987.

Hudson, Dolores. *Solving Writing Problems with Easy Mini-lessons*. Huntington Beach, CA: Creative Teaching Press, Inc., 1999.

Graves, Donald. *A Fresh Look At Writing*. Portsmouth, NH: Heinemann, 1994.

Johnson, Bea. *Never Too Early to Write*. Gainesville, FL: Maupin House, 1999.

Hindley, Joanne. *In the Company of Children*. Portland, MA: Stenhouse, 1996.

McElveen, Susan Anderson and Connie Campbell Dierking. *Literature Models to Teach Expository Writing*. Gainesville, FL: Maupin House, 2001.

Miller, Debbie. *Reading With Meaning*. Portland, MA: Stenhouse, 2002.

Pinnell, Gay Su, Irene Fountas, and Andrea McCarrier. *Interactive Writing*. Portsmouth, NH: Heinemann, 2000.

Ray, Katie Wood. *What You Know By Heart*. Portsmouth, NH: Heinemann, 2002.

Ray, Katie Wood. *Wondrous Words*. Urbana, IL: NCTE, 1999.

About the Authors

Connie Dierking (left) is originally from northeast Kansas. She holds a Bachelor's degree in Elementary Education and a Master's degree in Special Education, both from Kansas State University. During the past 24 years, Connie has experienced the joys of teaching kindergarten, second grade, third grade, and exceptional education students. She is involved in the Pinellas County Center for Learning Student Achievement Institute, a research and development program that supports classroom research in Best Practices. She is also a writing demonstration teacher for Pinellas County Schools.

Connie conducts reading and writing workshops throughout the United States. She is a co-author of two teacher resource books, *Teaching Writing Skills with Children's Literature* and *Literature Models to Teach Expository Writing*. She lives in Palm Harbor, Florida with her husband and two daughters. Connie teaches first grade at Curtis Fundamental Elementary in Clearwater, Florida.

Sherra Jones earned a Bachelor's Degree in Elementary Education from the University of South Florida. She is a charter member of the Classroom Learning System Cadre which trains teachers in Best Practices for classroom implementation. She conducts writing training for teachers and parents on reading and writing strategies. Her 20 years of teaching include preschool, kindergarten, and first grade. She teaches first grade at Curtis Fundamental Elementary in Clearwater, Florida, where she lives with her husband and two daughters.

If you liked *Growing Up Writing*, try these other Maupin House resources.

Teaching Writing Skills with Children's Literature

Connie Campbell Dierking and Susan Anderson McElveen

Teach brainstorming, focus, organization, elaboration and writing conventions using literature as models. Primary- and intermediate-level lessons for each of twenty models allow you to customize your writing workshops to the needs and abilities of your K-5 students.

ISBN 0-929895-27-4, 176 pp. Bibliography. Item #MH 43 • $19.95

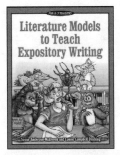

Literature Models to Teach Expository Writing

Susan Anderson McElveen and Connie Campbell Dierking

Model and demonstrate target skills critical for clear expository writing: description, explaining how and why, writing leads and endings, describing cause and effect, comparing and contrasting, and differentiating fact from opinion. Kindergarten, primary, and intermediate lessons for each literature selection help you integrate content-area writing throughout your curriculum.

ISBN 0-929895-47-9, 212 pp. Bibliography. Item #MH 76 • $23.95

Research in the Real Classroom: The Independent Investigation
Method for Primary Students

Virginia Morse and Cindy Nottage

Want research projects that inspire more learning and cause less frustration? *Research in the Real Classroom* shows you how to walk students through every phase of the research process. Based on the Independent Investigation Method (IIM), a seven-step model that teaches kids the fundamentals of research, this primary level book is the first in the *Research in the Real Classroom* series. Research projects will never be the same!

ISBN 0-929895-55-X, Item #MH 97 • $19.95

Research in the Real Classroom shows you how easy it is to turn your existing units into research units. The completed thematic templates for the Primary Level make getting started simple. Lessons for each step of the research process are provided and made appropriate for every primary student.

At the Primary Level, the following thematic units are available ($13.95 each):

- **Insects (#MH 100) • Plants (#MH 102) • Rainforests (#MH 104)**
- **Magnets (#MH 101) • Presidents (#MH 103) • Solar Systems (#MH 105)**

(Continued on the following page.)

Never Too Early to Write

Adventures in the K-1 Writing Workshop

Bea Johnson

"Bea Johnson has hit a home run! Never Too Early to Write is very informative and motivating. 'Must' reading for everyone proclaiming to use developmentally appropriate and integrated language arts practices." —Bob Kirschbaum, Elementary principal and national reading presenter, Spencer, IA

Improve reading readiness for kindergartners: start them writing! These ten effective writing-workshop strategies work in any literature-based setting or with any readiness series. A lovely and very useful resource.

ISBN 0-929895-31-2, 132 pp. Bibliography. Item #MH 47 • $14.95

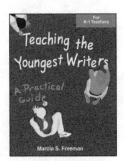

Teaching the Youngest Writers

A Practical Guide

Marcia S. Freeman

"…A well-written, valuable teaching resource, rich with classroom-tested models and writing techniques that emergent writers need." —Brenda Parkes, Ph.D., author and literacy consultant

This classic and complete writing workshop resource takes your primary students from emergent to elaborative writers. Includes models for managing the writing process and explains the expository, descriptive and personal narrative writing techniques your students need to become fluent writers.

ISBN 0-929895-26-6, 143 pp. Index, Bibliography. Item #MH 42 • $19.95

Non-fiction Writing Strategies

Using Science Big Books as Models

Marcia S. Freeman

"Using Big Books to integrate science and writing has worked wonders in my classroom. My students' writing shows significant and continual improvement as the enthusiastically respond to Marcia Freeman's well-organized and easy-to-implement lessons." —Idaho teacher

Here's how to use Newbridge Early Science Big Books—or any other Big Book series—as models of good writing to teach the information-writing techniques so critical for student success on performance-based writing tests. Includes strategies for teaching writing-craft fundamentals, oral and written models, student examples, practice activities, assessment procedures and advice on preparing young writers for success on performance-based tests.

ISBN 0-929895-37-1, 122 pp. Index, Bibliography. Item #MH 67 • $19.95

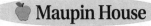

1-800-524-0634 • www.maupinhouse.com